RECIPES FROM A
TURKISH KITCHEN

RECIPES FROM A
TURKISH KITCHEN

TRADITIONS • INGREDIENTS • TASTES • TECHNIQUES

GHILLIE BAŞAN

For Yasmin and Zeki (the most special little people
in my world) *Afiyet olsun*!

This edition is published by Aquamarine,
an imprint of Anness Publishing Ltd,
Blaby Road, Wigston, Leicestershire
LE18 4SE; info@anness.com

www.aquamarinebooks.com;
www.annesspublishing.com

If you like the images in this book
and would like to investigate using
them for publishing, promotions or
advertising, please visit our website
www.practicalpictures.com
for more information.

Publisher: Joanna Lorenz
Project Editors: Doreen Gillon and Felicity
Forster Stylist: Helen Trent
Food Stylist: Lucy McKelvie
Designer: Green Tangerine

© Anness Publishing Ltd 2013

Author's acknowledgements
Having spent vast chunks of my adult life
visiting, or writing about, Turkey, there are
always many people to thank for their
assistance and hospitality. I must mention
my good friend Hasan Selamet in Istanbul,
who is always unfailingly helpful and keeps
me up to date with what is new.

This book would not have been possible
without the patience of Yasmin and Zeki
and their appetite for Turkish food. My
thanks also go to Peter for putting up with
the disruption of home life, and to my
parents, who are never far away and
always understanding. I would also like to
thank my wonderful editor Jeni Wright,
and Martin Brigdale for his sumptuous
photography.

Notes
Bracketed terms are intended for
American readers.
For all recipes, quantities are given in
both metric and imperial measures and,
where appropriate, in standard cups and
spoons. Follow one set of measures,
but not a mixture, because they
are not interchangeable.
Standard spoon and cup measures are level.
1 tsp = 5ml, 1 tbsp = 15ml, 1 cup =
250ml/8fl oz.
Australian standard tablespoons are 20ml.
Australian readers should use 3 tsp in place
of 1 tbsp for measuring small quantities.
American pints are 16fl oz/2 cups. American
readers should use 20fl oz/2.5 cups in place
of 1 pint when measuring liquids.
Electric oven temperatures in this book are
for conventional ovens. When using a fan
oven, the temperature will probably need
to be reduced by about 10–20°C/20–40°F.
Since ovens vary, you should check with
your manufacturer's instruction book
for guidance.
The nutritional analysis given for each recipe
is calculated per portion (i.e. serving or
item), unless otherwise stated. If the recipe
gives a range, such as Serves 4–6, then the
nutritional analysis will be for the smaller
portion size, i.e. 6 servings. The analysis
does not include optional ingredients, such
as salt added to taste.
Medium (US large) eggs are used unless
otherwise stated.
Front cover shows Chargrilled Sardines in
Vine Leaves – for recipe, see page 104

contents

6   ancient traditions, contemporary cuisine

8   a taste of Turkey

10   the traditional kitchen

16   traditional drinks

18   meze and salads

42   soups and hot snacks

62   vegetarian and vegetable dishes

82   pilaffs, beans and lentils

100   fish and shellfish

118   meat and poultry

138   sweet snacks and jams

158   index

ancient traditions, contemporary cuisine

Diverse, fascinating and steeped in history, Turkey boasts a peaceful landscape dotted with impressive mosques, ancient Roman ruins, colourful markets and rustic villages. With one foot in Europe and the other in Asia, Turkey acts as a geographical and cultural bridge between the two continents, a fact that is so vividly evident in the country's cuisine.

Above *The Suleymaniye mosque, overlooking the Bosphorus, is one of Istanbul's most famous landmarks.*

Within Turkey, the two continents are divided by the Bosphorus, the waterway that flows through the middle of Istanbul, once the seat of the Ottoman Empire, and still the centre of commerce and trade today. Anatolia, the Asian heartland, is the country's food bowl. Surrounded by the Black Sea, the Aegean and the Mediterranean, and linked by two wide straits, the Çanakkale (Dardanelles) and the Bosphorus, with the Sea of Marmara in between, Anatolia is blessed with a wealth of fish and shellfish, including freshwater varieties from the many rivers. Inland, climatic variations are striking, with long winters gripping the east and hot summers the south. Divided by high mountains and fertile central plains, this region boasts plentiful crops of fruit and vegetables, and rich pastures for cattle and sheep.

culinary influences

The ancestors of the Turks migrated from the Altay mountains in central Asia and drifted towards Anatolia, meeting different culinary traditions on their way, some based on animal products, such as the milk and meat of their horses, as well as the wild animals they hunted. When they reached Anatolia, they found a rich heritage based on beans, wheat, lentils and salt cooked with oil extracted from plants. As each group of peoples – Hittites, Romans, Byzantines, Arabs, Mongols and Crusaders – crossed Anatolia from east to west, they added to the culinary pool, thereby enriching the indigenous Turks' own cultural characteristics and cooking techniques.

Following the death of the Prophet Muhammad in AD632, the spread of Islamic culture throughout the Middle East had a lasting effect on Turkey. As the Golden Age of Islam flourished with Baghdad as its capital, the Arabs invaded and conquered vast territories, imposing religious restrictions on all aspects of the cultures they encountered. By the 11th century, migrating Turks gained in strength and formed a warrior aristocracy, resulting in the establishment of the Seljuk (Selçuk) Empire in Konya. The culinary culture of this period was influenced by the sophisticated cuisine of Persia, recorded by the poet and mystic

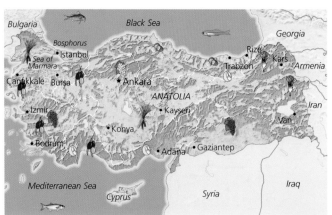

Left *With one foot in Europe and the other in Asia, Turkey acts as a geographical and cultural bridge between the two continents.*

Mevlana Celaleddin Rumi, who listed many recipes using vegetables, such as leeks, spinach and turnip, and pilaff and kebab dishes that are still cooked today. It was around this time that the Turks began to understand the importance of eating healthily, devising a system of balancing the warming and cooling properties of foods based on the ancient Chinese principles of Yin and Yang.

the Palace cuisine
The most significant impact on Turkish cuisine came during the Ottoman (Osmanlı) Empire, which was established in the 14th century. Once Constantinople (Istanbul) had been conquered by Mehmet II in 1453, the Topkapı Palace became the centre of the Empire and all culinary activity. Mehmet II was a gourmet with a penchant for indulging in lavish feasts prepared by carefully selected chefs. During his reign (AD1451–81), the Palace kitchens boasted a huge staff of specialist chefs, such as the *börekçi* (savoury pastry maker) and the *baklavacı* (sweet pastry maker), resulting in a plethora of creative dishes that became known as the Palace (*Saray*) cuisine.

As the Ottoman Empire expanded during its six-century rule, it also increased its culinary repertoire by flamboyantly adopting and adapting the recipes it encountered in the Balkans, the Mediterranean region, North Africa and much of the Arab world. During the reign of Süleyman the Magnificent (AD1520–66), the creations from the Palace kitchens reached such dizzy heights of indulgence that dishes emerged with sensuous names such as "young girls' breasts", and "ladies'

Right A goatherd and his flock beneath Mount Ararat.

thighs", specialities that are still part of Istanbul's cuisine today. Cooking was regarded as an art form and eating a pleasure, a legacy that remains at the root of Turkish cooking.

In the 16th and 17th centuries, the Ottomans persuaded the Spaniards, the other key players at that time, to return from the New World via the North African coast, so that new ingredients like chilli peppers, tomatoes and maize could be brought into Constantinople. These new ingredients were quickly absorbed into the Palace cuisine, from where they filtered throughout the Empire, shaping much of the Mediterranean diet as we know it today.

When the Ottoman Empire collapsed at the end of World War I, its culinary influence was evident to the west of Constantinople, but as the Empire had never really penetrated eastwards into the heart of Anatolia, the local Anatolian dishes survived there in their simplicity.

a divided cuisine
The cuisine of modern Turkey is therefore a divided one, founded on its ancient Anatolian traditions and its

Above *Colourful markets selling all kinds of fruit, vegetables and other produce can be found everywhere in Turkey, and it is customary to buy fresh ingredients every day.*

sophisticated Ottoman heritage. Added to this, the Turks themselves are split between those who do not sway from traditional recipes and cooking methods, and those who are bursting with such creative flair that they are constantly coming up with something new and exciting. In essence, that is what Turkey and Turkish cuisine is all about – always developing, but never forgetting the ancient traditions.

Left Turkish delight for sale in the market in the old town in Istanbul. Sweet foods are very popular in Turkey, and are taken as a gift when visiting someone's home.

a taste of Turkey

Everywhere you turn in Turkey there is something to eat. Bread rings covered in sesame seeds; deep-fried mussels with garlic sauce; pastries bathed in syrup; divine milky puddings and chewy ice cream; vegetables stuffed, grilled and fried in endless ways; whole grilled fish sandwiched between two slabs of bread; pungent spices that set your mouth tingling; fresh herbs sold like bunches of flowers; ruby-red pomegranates and juicy ripe peaches that dribble down your chin ... this is a cuisine that is out of this world.

The Turks are masters at successfully combining three of the most important things in life: food, family and friends. Hospitality is high on the agenda, coming naturally to most Turks, and the concept of sharing is prevalent when friends, relatives and even strangers visit a Turkish home. Guests usually arrive with a gift of something sweet, then whatever there is to eat in the house is shared. Visiting, entertaining and eating are such an important part of Turkish culture that sayings like "Guests must eat what they find, not what they hope for!" and "Greet a Turk and be sure you will eat" are commonplace.

Traditional culinary customs still play an important role in parts of rural Anatolia, although among modern Turks many of these are dying out. Traditionally, meals were eaten at low tables, which were simply large round trays that the family sat around on cushions. The food was laid on the table in wide bowls and copper dishes, and everyone ate from them. In wealthy homes, family meals usually began with a soup, followed by a savoury pastry or pilaff and a vegetable dish, but in poorer households, there might only be one dish. Families still eat like this in rural Anatolia, but in modern, urban homes table arrangements mirror those of homes all over Europe.

Communal meals were traditionally eaten by men living in institutions – for example in the military, dervish lodges and rest houses. A bowl of soup or rice was placed in the middle of the low table and each diner was equipped with a spoon to dip in. The meal would end with a prayer and a pinch of salt on the tongue to thank God for the food. Soup and bread were the basic foods eaten communally, which meant the soup had to be wholesome and nourishing.

Right A typical interior of an Ottoman house, with a low table for eating traditional meals.

etiquette

Various rules of etiquette are observed when eating in a traditional Turkish home. Hands must be washed before and after the meal, and a prayer recited before and after eating. Two hands are used to break bread, while only three fingers are used to pass the food to the mouth. Any coughing, sneezing or picking of the teeth with a toothpick must be done with the head turned away from the table and the mouth covered with a hand. A pinch of salt is often eaten before and after the meal. It is also polite at the end of a meal to compliment the cook on the delicious food by saying *elinize sağlık* – health to your hands – the idea being that such gifted hands have produced a stunning spread and long may that last.

holy festivals and family celebrations

Most social and religious events would be unthinkable without some sort of gathering around food and drink. One of the principal religious feasts is *Ramazan Bayramı*, a three-day celebration of feasting at the end of the month of *Ramazan* (Ramadan), when every devout Muslim has to abstain from eating and drinking between sunrise and sunset. The meals served during *Ramazan* generally consist of light soups, seasonal vegetables cooked in olive oil, stuffed vine leaves and peppers, meat stews, and flat breads such as *pide* (pitta) and *güllaç* (paper-thin sheets of pastry soaked in milky rose-flavoured syrup). In addition to the festive savoury dishes at *Ramazan Bayramı*, sweet pastries, such as *baklava*, *kadayif* and *helva* and other forms of confectionery, are eaten in vast quantities and presented to guests, hosts and friends. No wonder its popular name is *Şeker Bayramı* – Festival of Sweets.

Kurban Bayramı, which marks the near sacrifice of Isaac, is celebrated with the ritual sacrifice of a ram. The meat from the ram is cooked in a variety of ways, such as tripe soup, stews, kebabs and pilaffs made with the liver, so nothing is wasted. Meat from the ram is also given to the poor in the neighbourhood.

Muharram, the first month of the Islamic calendar, is celebrated from the tenth day onwards, with a large bowl of *aşure*, a fruit and grain pudding that is shared with friends and neighbours. There are also four feast days known as *kandil*, at which *lokum* (Turkish delight), pastries soaked in syrup, *baklava*, *helva* and other sweet snacks are shared.

In some parts of Turkey the spring festival *Hıdrellez* is celebrated with picnic food such as stuffed vine leaves, *köfte* and pilaff dishes containing chunks of meat. The saffron-scented rice pudding, *zerde*, is served at weddings along with *helva* and *baklava*, in the belief that by eating something sweet, a sweet life will be ensured. A red drink, *lohusa şerbeti*, is drunk after the birth of a child, and

Above *Sweet pastries such as baklava are served at feasts for weddings, funerals, circumcisions and religious festivals.*

sweet pastries and *helva* are prepared for circumcisions and funerals as well as births. Even visits to the *hamam* – the communal Turkish bath – can involve cooking in some parts of Anatolia, as women and children gather together to bathe and eat picnic food.

Below *Almonds are a popular ingredient in sweet dishes such as sütlü nüriye – layers of syrupy pastry filled with shaved almonds. This family from a small rural village in south-west Turkey makes a living from growing almonds.*

the traditional kitchen

Red pepper from Gaziantep, tart green olives from Bodrum, dried apricots from Cappadocia, anchovy pilaff from Trabzon, spicy kebabs from Adana, hallucinogenic honey from Kars, creamy milk puddings and syrupy pastries – these are the tastes of the Turkish kitchen.

Food shopping in Turkish markets is a delight, and haggling is the name of the game. Daily and weekly shops are highly organized. Fruit, vegetables, herbs and spices are bought at the markets, as are nuts, dried fruit, olives, pickles, cheese and yogurt. Fish is bought from the fish market, while meat is most often bought at the butcher's. Puddings come from the pudding shop, pastries from the pastry shop, and bread from the baker's. Outside Turkey, most of the ingredients you need to cook Turkish food can be found in Middle Eastern, Mediterranean and health food stores, or at Turkish food centres.

Below With its long coastline Turkey has plentiful supplies of fish.

Above Spices are much used in Turkish cooking, and are bought from stalls in the markets.

Yin and Yang

From the days of the Seljuk Empire, when the ancient Chinese theory of Yin and Yang filtered into Turkish cuisine, the art of balancing the warming and cooling properties of certain foods developed in the traditional kitchen. Warming spices such as cumin, cinnamon, allspice, cloves and Turkish red pepper are used for stimulating the appetite and to aid digestion, while generous quantities of fresh herbs, particularly mint, dill and flat leaf parsley, are often mixed together as a warming triad to balance the cooling properties of certain vegetable dishes and salads. Pungent garlic, which is used liberally in eastern and southern Anatolia but added in subtle amounts to Ottoman dishes, is believed to be beneficial to the circulation of the blood.

Turkish red pepper

Kırmızı biber, Turkish red pepper, is a type of horn chilli that came from the New World. It has been grown in Turkey for several centuries and as a spice is in a class of its own. It is integral to *güney* cuisine, the cooking of southern Turkey, and is used liberally in Gaziantep.

Used with pride, *kırmızı biber* could be regarded as the Turkish national spice, but it comes in so many different forms and strengths that even the Turks find it confusing. The red chilli peppers are easy to recognize in Turkish markets, hung up on string in their fresh and dried forms, but you can also get them roughly chopped, crushed or flaked, or ground into a powder. The colour varies too, from vermilion to deep blood red and almost black when roasted. The best quality is ready-oiled so that it imparts its flavour immediately, even in uncooked

dishes. Very finely ground *pul biber* is the hottest of the lot, and should be used sparingly. In recipes you will find paprika or chilli suggested as substitutes for Turkish red pepper, but nothing tastes quite like the real thing.

olives

The Turks enjoy olives throughout the day, kicking off with a handful for breakfast to accompany a slab of *beyaz peynir*, the ubiquitous white cheese. These may then be followed by a few olives plucked from a market stall while shopping, a bowlful of marinated, plump ones as a snack or *meze* dish in the middle of the day, and then again in the evening. Olives are grown all over Turkey, producing a wide variety of colourful fruits – from purple to red, green, brown and black. After

harvesting, the young black olives are immersed in salt for a week, which makes the skins crinkle and the flesh soften. Rinsed of salt and stored in olive oil, these wrinkled black olives are

Above left and above Olives and red pepper are two of the most popular and familiar ingredients in Turkish cuisine. Both are widely grown all over Turkey.

popular for breakfast and snacks, while for a *meze* dish, olives often have lemon juice squeezed over them to enhance their taste. Olive stones have a purpose too – cleaned and polished smooth, they are threaded on strings to make prayer beads, *tespih*.

oils

Olive and sunflower oils are home-produced and used interchangeably, or together, for cooking. Olive oil is almost always used when the flavour of the oil is required to contribute to a dish, such as in the Palace *zeytinyağlı* vegetable dishes, casserole-style dishes and salads. In parts of rural Anatolia, clarified butter, or ghee, is used for meat and rice dishes, while the Turks and Kurds of the eastern region still enjoy the rancid flavour of *kuyrukyağı* (sheep's tail fat).

Left Local women sorting olives after the harvest. Olive trees are very hardy and manage to survive in poor soil in varied climates. At harvest time the trees are shaken so that the olives fall on to sheets placed on the ground.

Left A cheese stall in a local market selling all types of cow's and sheep's cheeses.

Eaten on its own as a snack, thick, creamy yogurt is often dusted with icing (confectioners') sugar, or drizzled with amber honey. Plain, it is served in dollops with vegetable and kebab dishes, or mixed with the mashed or grated pulp of cooked vegetables to make dips. Beaten with crushed garlic and a splash of lemon juice or vinegar, it is generously spooned over deep-fried or grilled (broiled) vegetables and poached eggs.

Everyday dishes include *cacık* (diced cucumber, yogurt, garlic and mint or dill), which is often served as an appetizer or as an accompaniment to savoury pastries and kebabs; *haydari*, a very thick yogurt dip spiked with garlic and fresh or dried mint; and *ayran*, the national, cooling yogurt drink, enjoyed with spicy food or as a thirst-quencher on a hot day.

The standard, everyday yogurt *sıvı tas* is thick, light and creamy, whereas the solid yogurt *süzme,* which is required for

cheese

There are many varieties of white cheese made from cow's or sheep's milk.

The principal, everyday white cheese, *beyaz peynir*, is fairly solid and sold in blocks. Stored in brine, it varies in its saltiness, so the first thing a cook does to draw out the salt is to immerse the block in water and keep it in a cool place. This cheese is eaten for breakfast with olives, bread and jam, and it is used in salads and savoury pastries. It is also served by itself as a *meze* dish – cubes are served drizzled with olive oil and sprinkled with dried oregano and Turkish red pepper or paprika. Feta is a good substitute for *beyaz peynir*.

A slightly softer, creamier white cheese than *beyaz peynir* is *köy peyniri*, "village cheese" which is made every week. The regional variations are much sought-after in the markets. Other cheeses include the hard and tangy *kaşar peyniri*, which is used in cooking and for grating on top of dishes, and *dil peyniri,* a mild-tasting cheese which is pulled apart in stringy strips and enjoyed with pickles.

yogurt

The Turks are one of the world's largest consumers of yogurt or *yoğurt*, which they generally prefer full-fat and made from ewe's milk. Once a staple of their ancestors in central Asia, yogurt is loved so much that it is served with almost everything, providing an easily digestible source of calcium, as well as vitamins, minerals and antibiotic properties.

Left Cheese is eaten for breakfast or as a meze dish, and used in cooking.

Ayran

If it is a very hot day when you make this drink, add a little extra salt and some ice cubes.

300ml/½ pint/1¼ cups thick and creamy natural (plain) yogurt

a pinch of salt

dried mint

SERVES 2

1 Whisk the yogurt in a jug (pitcher) with 300ml/½ pint/1¼ cups cold water until it becomes foamy. Season to taste with salt.

2 Pour into glasses, sprinkle with a little mint and serve immediately.

bove *Yogurt is served with almost everything, and the Turks prefer it thick and creamy.*

Above *A stack of jars in a pickle-shop window makes a colourful display.*

particular dips and puddings, is strained through a piece of muslin (cheesecloth) for about 6 hours so that it is so thick you can stand a spoon in it. For the recipes in this book, use a thick and creamy natural (plain) yogurt – the live "bio" and organic varieties are particularly good, and there are many to choose from in the supermarket.

pickles

In Turkey pickles take on a whole new meaning – they are not just for tucking into a sandwich or prodding with a cocktail stick (toothpick). A kaleidoscope of colour, the jars stacked in pickle-shop windows beckon passers-by to stop and choose their favourite pickle by the kilo, or quench their thirst with a glass of *turşu suyu,* pickle juice. In the autumn, market stalls are stocked with rock salt, garlic and celery – the chief elements required for pickle making – and small, unripe vegetables and fruit destined for the pickling pan: their acidity contributes to the fermentation process and they keep hard and crunchy, which is the way

they like them in Turkey. Nowadays, brine and wine vinegar are the standard pickling agents but, in the past, pickle merchants used fresh grape juice, which inevitably turned to vinegar during fermentation. Yeast, provided by a few chickpeas or mustard seeds, or by a slice of stale bread wrapped in muslin (cheesecloth), is sometimes added to the pickling jar to speed up the process.

Recipes like *patlıcan turşusu,* stuffed aubergine (eggplant) pickle, unchanged in method since the 15th century, are always a delight on the *meze* table. Other traditional pickles include white or red cabbage leaves, green tomatoes, turnip with a little beetroot (beet) to colour it pink, long, twisted green chilli peppers as well as the tiny, fiery ones, whole garlic, and unripe apricots, melons and pears, often mixed with immature green almonds.

When making your own Turkish pickles, store them in glass jars or stoneware crocks and taste the vinegar during the fermentation process to make sure it has retained its acidity.

Armut turşusu

Most Turkish pickles are sour or piquant to taste, but there are several sweet-and-sour ones that are delicious served with roasted or grilled (broiled) meat, and with cheese. This recipe for pickled pears with saffron, honey and spices is popular in the agricultural regions around Bursa, where the orchards provide plentiful harvests every year.

400ml/14fl oz/1²/₃ cups white wine, or cider vinegar

175g/6oz/³/₄ cup aromatic honey (rosemary, lavender or pine forest)

2 cinnamon sticks

8 allspice berries

a fingerful of saffron threads

4 firm pears, cut in half lengthways with the stalks intact, or 8 small, firm pears left whole

SERVES 4

1 Heat the vinegar in a large, heavy pan with 120ml/4fl oz/¹/₂ cup water, the honey, cinnamon, allspice and saffron. Bring the liquid to the boil, stirring all the time, until the honey has dissolved. Lower the heat, slip in the pears and poach gently for 15–20 minutes, until they are tender but still firm.

2 Lift the pears out of the pickling liquid and arrange them in a sterilized jar or crock. Pour the hot liquid over them and leave to cool. Cover the jar and store the pickled pears in a cool place, or in the refrigerator. Serve at room temperature or chilled.

bread

Regarded as the food of friendship, the Turks buy bread daily straight from the hot baker's oven. Torn apart with fingers, it is shared and eaten with every meal. Day-old bread is not wasted, but used in soups, *köfte* and nut *tarator*, and in popular puddings where it is soaked in syrup and often topped with poached fruits. Eaten as a snack, or with jam and white cheese for breakfast, bread is also indispensable at other meals, as a scoop or mop for all the tasty juices. In many households, a meal is unthinkable without bread, and if bread has to be thrown away, it is first kissed and held to the forehead as a mark of respect.

Both leavened and unleavened breads are popular in Turkey. The standard crusty leavened loaves, found in every village and town, are similar to baguettes in texture, but shaped like kayaks. Other leavened loaves include wholemeal (whole-wheat) and rye varieties, as well as the sesame-covered rings, *simit*, sold by street sellers who carry them through the crowds stacked on long poles, or on

Below A Turkish woman rolling out dough to make bread in the traditional way. This is still done in some remote villages.

wide, circular trays balanced on their heads. The principal flat breads are the paper-thin sheets of *yufka* and the soft, spongy *pide*. The local *yufkacı* is greatly valued for its daily supplies of freshly griddled *yufka*, ready for wrapping around fillings to make savoury pastries, or for layering with a filling like Italian lasagne. As the genuine article is difficult to obtain outside Turkey, filo is used as a substitute in the recipes in this book. There are many types of *pide* available at the local *fırın* (communal oven), such as the delicious, sweet *helva pide*, and the sesame-sprinkled *Ramazan pide*, which is eaten to break the fast during the month of *Ramazan*. In some recipes, pitta breads are suggested as an alternative to *pide*, because they are so readily available in supermarkets and Middle Eastern stores, but if you have time to make fresh *pide*, it is worth it.

other essential ingredients

• Pine nuts, almonds and pistachios are added to many savoury and sweet dishes, while walnuts, the king of nuts, play a principal role in traditional *baklava* and *tarator* sauce.

Above A beekeeper collecting honey from his beehives in pine forests near Akyaka in south-western Turkey.

• Sesame seeds are sprinkled over breads, cakes and buns, and ground to a thick paste called *tahin*.

• Currants provide a sweet note in savoury fillings, stews and *köfte*.

• Saffron adds colour and flavour to ceremonial puddings.

• *Sumac* is ground from deep-red, sour berries. It is sprinkled over salads, savoury snacks and fish.

• Rose water lends its floral tones to sweet syrups and milk puddings.

• Vine leaves are used for wrapping and layering. They are sold fresh, dried or preserved in brine.

• Vanilla pods and extract are used as flavouring for milky puddings.

• *Mastika*, an aromatic resin, creates a chewy texture in ice cream, milk puddings and *rakı*.

• Honey is believed to sweeten life and keep sadness at bay. The fiery *deli bal* honey from Kars creates a mild hallucinatory sensation.

Pide

This tasty *pide* can be enjoyed with any savoury dish in this book. Hot from the oven, it is delicious drizzled with honey.

15g/½oz fresh yeast, or 7g/¼ oz active dried yeast

2.5ml/½ tsp sugar

450g/1lb/4 cups unbleached strong white bread flour

5ml/1 tsp salt

about 150ml/¼ pint/⅔ cup lukewarm water

30ml/2 tbsp olive oil, plus a few extra drops

30ml/2 tbsp natural (plain) yogurt

1 egg, beaten

15ml/1 tbsp nigella, or sesame, seeds

MAKES 2 MEDIUM, OR 1 LARGE, PIDE

1 Mix the yeast and sugar in a small bowl with 30–45ml/2–3 tbsp of the lukewarm water. Set aside for about 15 minutes, until frothy.

2 Sift the flour and salt into a bowl. Make a well in the middle and pour in the creamed yeast with 30ml/2 tbsp oil, the yogurt and remaining water. Using your hands, draw in the flour from the sides and work the mixture into a dough, until it leaves the side of the bowl.

3 Turn the dough out on to a lightly floured surface and knead until smooth and light. Punch it flat, then gather up the edges into the middle and flip it over. Splash a few drops of oil in the bottom of a large bowl, roll the ball of dough in it, and cover with a damp dish towel. Leave the dough in a warm place for a few hours, or overnight, until it has doubled in size.

4 Preheat the oven to 220°C/425°F/Gas 7. Punch the dough down to release the air, then knead again. Lightly oil a large baking tray and pop it in the oven for 2 minutes.

5 Place the dough on a floured surface and flatten it with the heel of your hand. Use your fingers to stretch it from the middle, creating a thick lip at the edges. Indent the dough with your fingertips and place it on the baking tray. Brush with a little beaten egg and sprinkle over the nigella or sesame seeds.

6 Bake for about 20 minutes, until the surface is crispy and golden. Transfer to a wire rack and serve warm, tearing it roughly with your fingers.

temperatures and cooking times for dishes such as milk puddings, *helva*, sweet pastries and *lokum* (Turkish delight), but traditional Turkish kitchens in ordinary homes are very simple, relying on skilful hands and nimble fingers rather than on any special equipment. Around the kitchen hearth or stove in rural Anatolia, you will see only a few basic tools – wooden spoons, heavy pans, a copper, tin-lined yogurt urn and a sturdy mortar and pestle.

In many rural villages a communal oven, *fırın*, is used for baking bread and pastry doughs, while city dwellers rely on the neighbourhood specialist bakers for their breads and pastries.

For festive occasions, a whole sheep or goat may be cooked in a pit dug in the ground, otherwise cuts of meat and fish are often cooked on a *mangal*, a portable charcoal-fired barbecue that can be used on the balcony of an apartment, in the garden, on the beach, or out in the countryside for a family picnic.

Below Fish are sometimes cooked on a mangal, a portable charcoal-fired barbecue that can be taken on a picnic. Whole fish will often be eaten sandwiched between two slabs of bread.

utensils and equipment

Traditional Turkish cooking utensils are quite splendid, and you will see many of them in museums throughout the country. Communal meals in institutions were prepared in huge cauldrons, each one different according to the place where they were used. Spoons were of great significance, shrouded in such sayings as "Fate turns up in the spoon." They came in different shapes and sizes, some of them carved out of wood or tortoiseshell, other more grand ones made of silver, gold or mother-of-pearl, often inset with precious gems.

Chefs trained in the Palace cuisine require sophisticated utensils, and they need to be accurate with oven

traditional drinks

Tea is the most popular drink in Turkey, and it is drunk all year round and all day long – it could be regarded as the national drink. Coffee is more expensive, and making it is an art form that is taken seriously. Alcohol is prohibited to Muslims, but many Turks drink locally produced *rakı*, wine and beer.

Şerbet, made from fruit syrup or from syrups made with rose petals, orange blossom, honey, almonds and tamarind, is a cool and refreshing drink for the summer. In winter, a warming drink is *boza*, a thick mixture made from fermented bulgur that is served sprinkled with cinnamon. Glasses of the pale yellow liquid are lined up in pudding-shop windows, and carts laden with large copper jugs (pitchers) of *boza* are pulled through the streets as the seller calls out for custom. Also popular in the winter is *salep*, which is made from the ground root of orchids. Thick, milky and sweet, and dusted with a little cinnamon, it is warming and nourishing.

alcohol

Before the advent of Islam, the Turks enjoyed a variety of alcoholic drinks, such as crude beers, wines and fermented mare's milk, *kımız*, all collectively known as *çakır* (*çakırkeyif* means "tipsy") and usually accompanied by *meze* dishes. Alcoholic drinks were prohibited with the conversion to Islam, and many Muslims adhere strictly to the rules, but there are also many Turks who drink alcohol. Wines and beers are produced locally, but top of the alcohol list is the aniseed-flavoured drink *rakı*, which turns cloudy when water is added and is often referred to as "lion's milk".

tea

The drinking of tea, *çay*, is big business in Turkey. There are *çay* houses in every village, on every city street, at ports and stations and near busy office buildings. The sight of young boys and men carrying trays of tea glasses through crowds or across busy roads is a common one, as tea is served throughout the day to passers-by, gatherings of friends and thirsty office staff. Tea is offered to you in banks while you wait, in shops and markets as you browse, in meetings of any description, and in houses when you are welcomed. It is a drink of friendship and hospitality, and it is polite to accept.

Tea is invariably served in tulip-shaped glasses, a legacy of Sultan Ahmet III (1703–30), who encouraged the design of tulips on tiles and other artefacts. Traditionally it was made in a bulky copper samovar, but nowadays it is made in a modern tin or aluminium version that consists of a small teapot containing the tea resting on a larger teapot containing the water. The tea leaves are usually home-grown, mainly from plantations at Rize on the Black Sea coast, and the tea is made strong. It is served with lumps of sugar, which some people stir in while others place them in their mouths and suck the tea through them. It is never drunk with milk.

coffee

A more prestigious and expensive drink than tea, the first small cup of *kahve* is enjoyed at the start of the day, the second cup is drunk mid-morning, and a third may be drunk after a long meal. As it is more expensive than tea, coffee is not available to all on a daily basis. In some Anatolian communities, where coffee is reserved for special occasions only, the tradition still exists of selecting a bride according to her coffee-making skills – her prospective husband and his

Left Drinking tea is an elegant occasion, with the tulip-shaped glasses and bowl of sugar. It is offered to welcome guests, as a sign of hospitality.

mother judge her not only for her beauty but also for her ability to prepare coffee.

Turkish coffee is traditionally made in a *cezve* – a slim, deep pot with a long handle – often made out of tin-lined copper. Generally, medium-roast Arabica coffee beans are passed through a very fine grinder until almost powdery. Some specialist coffee shops have a Turkish setting on their grinding machines, but

Above Turkish men spend many hours in the local teahouse, where they drink endless cups of tea and play games such as backgammon and dominoes.

this often doesn't grind the beans fine enough, so you should ask for it to be passed through the machine several times. Most Turks drink their coffee sweet, but you can drink it *sade* (plain and unsweetened), *orta şekerli* (medium sweet) or *şekerli* (sweet).

Above Coffee is generally served in small white cups, and the Turks prefer it very sweet and without the addition of milk.

Below Rakı is the preferred alcoholic drink. The clear liquid turns cloudy when water is added to dilute it.

the art of making Turkish coffee

- Measure the water by the coffee cup – small, after-dinner size – and the coffee by the teaspoon. For medium-sweet coffee, allow one coffee cup of water to one teaspoon of coffee and one teaspoon of sugar per person.
- Tip the water into the *cezve* and spoon the coffee and sugar on top. Using a teaspoon, quickly stir the sugar and coffee across the surface of the water to kick-start a froth.
- Put the pot over a medium heat. Using the teaspoon, slowly scrape across the surface of the coffee in a

circular motion, working from the outside into the middle to create an island of froth. The key to good froth is to always work on the surface, never touching the bottom of the pot with a spoon.
- Once the coffee is hot, pour about a third of it into the coffee cup to warm the cup up. Return the pot to the heat and continue gathering the froth in the middle. After a few seconds, just as the coffee begins to bubble up, take it off the heat and pour it into the cup.
- Leave the coffee to stand for a minute, to let the grains settle, then drink it while it is hot.

MEZE AND SALADS

taze ezmesi

tahin tarama

smoked aubergine and yogurt purée

kısır

carrot and caraway purée with yogurt

acvar

muhammara

baked chickpea purée with lemon
and pine nuts

stir-fried spinach with currants, pine nuts
and yogurt

bean salad with red onion, eggs, olives
and anchovies

gypsy salad with feta, chillies and parsley

celery and coconut salad with lime

grated beetroot and yogurt salad

meze and salads

Adaptable as nibbles, appetizers, snacks, or a buffet spread, Turkish *meze* and salads are delicious and infinite in variety – there are said to be over 40 dishes with aubergines alone.

The wonderful thing about *meze* is that there are no rules. Often loosely translated as hors d'oeuvres, appetizer or snack, *meze* is so versatile that it can be all of these things and more. The literal translation is "pleasant taste" and that is just what *meze* is – something tasty.

Traditionally, a table of *meze* was laid out to accompany *rakı*, with the aim of achieving a "pleasant head" – to delight the palate, not fill the belly – and the relaxed enjoyment of *meze* was often accompanied by feelings of peace and serenity, even deep meditation. It was a custom enjoyed by men, most often traders and travellers, but over time it has evolved into a family affair. The *meze* table has never been regulated by time or order, just the unspoken understanding that the food should be served in small quantities, to be savoured and shared at a leisurely pace. With this in mind, many Turks like to eat *meze* with a glass of cloudy *rakı* in the evening, when time is not pressing.

Above, from left to right
Pide, *baked tomatoes, baked chickpea purée.*

There are those who insist that only a bowl or plate of nuts, olives or small pieces of fruit is a true *meze*, while others feel it can be anything and everything, from warm, freshly toasted pumpkin seeds to small, succulent kebabs – even street food like peeled and salted cucumbers. For the purists who claim that *meze* should consist of just one fruit, each season offers its own special gems – fine slices of fresh quince with a squeeze of lemon, unripe and tart-tasting green plums (*erik*) dipped in salt, and large, ruby pomegranates dripping with juice. Fresh watermelons, cherries, apricots and figs are also popular *meze* fruits, but the most common fruit to accompany *rakı* has always been golden cubes of sweet, juicy melon, either served on their own or with cubes of white cheese.

The most primitive form of *meze* is a small plate of *çerez* – a dainty serving of dried fruit such as white mulberries, plump olives with a squeeze of lemon, or even just a selection of nuts, roasted pumpkin seeds, salted sunflower seeds or *leblebi* (roasted chickpeas – the traditional accompaniment to *rakı*).

Another simple form of *meze* is the popular *ezme*, which consists of ingredients that are beaten, crushed, mashed, pounded, puréed or pressed into a paste to make them the perfect

consistency for scooping up with bread or using as a dip. Not all pounded or puréed dishes are called *ezme* though – some have their own names, like *humus* made with chickpeas, *tarama* made with fish roe, and *fava*, a dish of puréed broad (fava) beans. Others come under the umbrella name of *salata* or salad.

Meze and salads go hand in hand, because many salads are served as *meze* and some dishes are called salads even if they do not look like them. Incredibly versatile, both *meze* and salads are suited to the Western way of eating, as a small assortment can be served as nibbles with drinks while a wide choice can be prepared for a buffet. A large *meze* spread can consist of a myriad of miniature foods, sometimes even miniature versions of a main dish, such as mini Anatolian pizzas (*fistic lahmacun*) or small meatballs (*cizbiz*).

Istanbul is home to some of the best *meze* and salads. In this vast, vibrant city, almost every regional variation can be found somewhere, ranging from the simple spicy tastes of Anatolia to the more elaborate dishes from the Palace kitchens of the Ottoman Empire. If you eat the same *meze* in its region of origin, however, it may be different again – in Amasya the *acı ezmesi* (hot pepper paste) can be so hot it blows your head off, whereas in Istanbul the chilli taste may be so mild that it only gives a faint nip to the tongue. Even in the shabbiest parts of the city, families will be seated in courtyards, doorways and on balconies, in fact anywhere they can set up a makeshift table to balance a few *meze* dishes.

One of life's little pleasures is to sit by the Bosphorus watching the boats slip hypnotically by, as you nibble and savour the lip-licking, flavoursome goodness of each tasty morsel, allowing time to stand still for *meze*.

Heavenly, garlic-flavoured, smoked aubergine (eggplant) purée; springy cracked wheat salad with tomato, mint and flat leaf parsley; crushed green olives with coriander seeds; small green (bell) peppers stuffed with aromatic rice, pine nuts and currants; spicy walnut purée with pomegranate syrup; artichokes and broad beans in olive oil; a sweet, tangy *tahin* and lemon purée; light, crisp, cigar-shaped pastries filled with white cheese, mint and dill; plump mussels coated in a beer batter and deep-fried; tiny tasty fish *köfte* flavoured with cinnamon and dill; thin strips of warm, grilled aubergine and courgette (zucchini) served with a cooling, garlic-flavoured yogurt; and whole, juicy mushrooms cooked with pine nuts, spices and fresh herbs. When thinking of *meze*, this is what comes to mind.

Above, from left to right
Feta cheese, bean salad with red onion, aubergines (eggplants).

taze ezmesi

The Turkish word *taze* means fresh, which is exactly what this *meze* dish is – a mixture of chopped fresh vegetables. Along with cubes of honey-sweet melon and feta, or plump, juicy olives spiked with red pepper and oregano, this is *meze* at its simplest and best. Popular in kebab houses, it makes a tasty snack or appetizer, and is good served with chunks of warm, crusty bread or toasted pitta.

turning the salad into a paste *When you bind the chopped vegetables with the olive oil, add 15–30ml/1–2 tbsp tomato purée (paste) with a little extra chilli and 5–10ml/1–2 tsp sugar. The mixture will become a tangy paste to spread on fresh, crusty bread or toasted pitta, and it can also be used as a sauce for grilled, broiled or barbecued meats.*

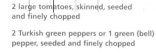

2 large tomatoes, skinned, seeded and finely chopped

2 Turkish green peppers or 1 green (bell) pepper, seeded and finely chopped

1 onion, finely chopped

1 green chilli, seeded and finely chopped

1 small bunch of fresh flat leaf parsley, finely chopped

a few fresh mint leaves, finely chopped

15–30ml/1–2 tbsp olive oil

salt and ground black pepper

SERVES 4

1 Put all the finely chopped ingredients in a bowl and mix well together.

2 Bind the mixture with oil and season with salt and pepper.

3 Serve at room temperature, in individual bowls or one large dish.

per portion Energy 101kcal/420kJ; Protein 2.3g; Carbohydrate 9.3g, of which sugars 8g; Fat 6.3g, of which saturates 0.9g; Cholesterol 0mg; Calcium 66mg; Fibre 2.7g; Sodium 15mg.

45ml/3 tbsp light sesame paste (*tahin*)

juice of 1 lemon

15–30ml/1–2 tbsp clear honey

5–10ml/1–2 tsp dried mint

lemon wedges, to serve

SERVES 2

1 Beat the sesame paste and lemon juice together in a bowl.

2 Add the honey and mint and beat again until thick and creamy, then spoon into a small dish.

3 Serve at room temperature, with lemon wedges for squeezing.

sweet treat *Popular for breakfast or as a sweet snack is tahin pekmez. Combine 30–45ml/2–3 tbsp light sesame paste with 30ml/2 tbsp grape molasses (pekmez) to form a sweet paste, then scoop up with chunks of fresh bread. If you can't find pekmez, use date syrup from Middle Eastern and health food stores.*

tahin tarama

This delightful little dip from central Anatolia is often served in outdoor cafés and restaurants as a *meze* dish on its own – a sort of whetting of the appetite while you wait for the assortment of exciting dishes to come. Sometimes you will see groups of old men drinking *rakı* or refreshing tea, sharing a plate of *tahin tarama* or a bowl of roasted chickpeas while they play cards or backgammon. Sweet and tangy, it is good mopped up with chunks of crusty bread or toasted pitta bread.

per portion Energy 160kcal/664kJ; Protein 4.3g; Carbohydrate 6.4g, of which sugars 6.2g; Fat 13.3g, of which saturates 1.9g; Cholesterol 0mg; Calcium 155mg; Fibre 1.8g; Sodium 6mg.

smoked aubergine and yogurt purée

One of the most popular *meze* dishes, this garlic-flavoured purée, *patlıcan ezmesi*, varies from house to house and region to region, sometimes made with a heavy hand of garlic or a kick of chilli, or with the fresh taste of dill, mint or parsley. It is heavenly when freshly made, served with chunks of crusty bread for scooping up.

2 large, plump aubergines (eggplants)

30ml/2 tbsp olive oil, plus extra for drizzling

juice of 1 lemon

2–3 garlic cloves, crushed

225g/8oz/1 cup thick and creamy natural (plain) yogurt

salt and ground black pepper

a few fresh dill fronds, to garnish

lemon wedges, to serve

SERVES 4

1 Put the aubergines directly on the gas flame on top of the stove, or under a conventional grill (broiler), and turn them from time to time until the skin is charred on all sides and the flesh feels soft. Place them in a plastic bag and leave for a few minutes.

2 Hold each aubergine by the stalk under cold running water and gently peel off the charred skin until you are left with just the smooth bulbous flesh. Squeeze the flesh with your fingers to get rid of any excess water and place it on a chopping board.

3 Chop the aubergine flesh to a pulp, discarding the stalks. Put the flesh in a bowl with 30ml/2 tbsp oil, the lemon juice and garlic. Beat well to mix, then beat in the yogurt and season with salt and pepper. Transfer to a bowl, drizzle with olive oil and garnish with dill. Serve at room temperature, with lemon wedges for squeezing.

to make a smoky salad *Toss the smoked aubergine flesh with the olive oil and lemon juice, some sliced spring onions (scallions), chopped tomatoes, parsley and dill, and you have* patlıcan salatası.

outdoor cooking *This is a great dish for a summer barbecue. Instead of charring the aubergines on the stove, lay them on the rack over hot charcoal and cook for 15–20 minutes, turning them from time to time until they are soft – the skin will remain firm, but the flesh will cook inside. Lift the aubergines off the rack, place on a chopping board and slit open lengthways with a sharp knife. Scoop out the flesh and chop to a pulp, then continue as above.*

per portion Energy 103kcal/431kJ; Protein 4.4g; Carbohydrate 7.7g, of which sugars 6.4g; Fat 6.5g, of which saturates 1.2g; Cholesterol 1mg; Calcium 118mg; Fibre 2.3g; Sodium 49mg.

kısır

This traditional *meze* dish of bulgur and tomato is easy to make and very tasty. Packed with fresh mint and parsley, it is both filling and refreshing. It is good served at room temperature as part of a buffet or barbecue spread, with lemon wedges for squeezing over it. In some Turkish households, *kısır* is offered to guests before tea is served. On these occasions, the *kısır* is spooned on to vine leaves and is accompanied by slices of tomato and some pickles.

175g/6oz/1 cup bulgur wheat, rinsed and drained

45–60ml/3–4 tbsp olive oil

juice of 1–2 lemons

30ml/2 tbsp tomato purée (paste)

10ml/2 tsp sugar

1 large or 2 small red onions, cut in half lengthways, in half again crossways, and sliced along the grain

10ml/2 tsp Turkish red pepper, or 1–2 fresh red chillies, seeded and finely chopped

1 bunch each of fresh mint and flat leaf parsley, finely chopped

salt and ground black pepper

a few fresh mint and parsley leaves, to garnish

SERVES 4–6

1 Put the bulgur into a wide bowl, pour over enough boiling water to cover it by about 2.5cm/1in, and give it a quick stir. Cover the bowl with a plate or pan lid and leave the bulgur to steam for about 25 minutes, until it has soaked up the water and doubled in quantity.

2 Pour the oil and lemon juice over the bulgur and toss to mix, then add the tomato purée and toss the mixture again until the bulgur is well coated.

3 Add the sugar, onion, Turkish red pepper or chillies, and the herbs. Season with salt and pepper.

4 Serve at room temperature, garnished with a little mint and parsley.

getting the flavours right *This salad should be light and lemony, packed full of the refreshing flavours of parsley and mint, with a slight tang of chilli, so be liberal with these ingredients. The sugar intensifies the tomato flavour of the purée.*

making a fiery *kısır* *In the south-east of Turkey, where the juice of sour pomegranates is often used instead of lemons and hot red pepper is added liberally to food, a fiery* kısır *is moulded into small balls and served in lettuce-leaf wrappings.*

per portion Energy 149Kcal/620kJ; Protein 3g; Carbohydrate 21.6g, of which sugars 5.4g; Fat 6.1g, of which saturates 0.8g; Cholesterol 0mg; Calcium 54mg; Fibre 1.7g; Sodium 19mg.

6 large carrots, thickly sliced

5ml/1 tsp caraway seeds

30–45ml/2–3 tbsp olive oil

juice of 1 lemon

225g/8oz/1 cup thick and creamy natural (plain) yogurt

1–2 garlic cloves, crushed

salt and ground black pepper

a few fresh mint leaves, to garnish

SERVES 4

carrot and caraway purée with yogurt

Long, thin carrots that are orange, yellow, red and purple are a colourful feature in the vegetable markets throughout Turkey. Used mainly in salads, lentil dishes and stews, they are also married with garlic-flavoured yogurt for *meze* – sliced and deep-fried drizzled with yogurt, grated and folded in, or steamed and puréed, then served with the yogurt in the middle, as in this recipe. Try serving the carrot purée while it is still warm, with chunks of crusty bread or warm pitta to scoop it up.

1 Steam the carrots for about 25 minutes, until they are very soft. While they are still warm, mash them to a smooth purée, or whiz them in a blender.

2 Beat the caraway seeds into the carrot purée, followed by the oil and lemon juice. Season with salt and pepper.

3 Beat the yogurt and garlic in a separate bowl, and season with salt and pepper. Spoon the warm carrot purée around the edge of a serving dish, or pile into a mound and make a well in the middle. Spoon the yogurt into the middle, and garnish with mint.

steaming vegetables *It is always best to steam, rather than boil, vegetables, so they retain their taste, texture and goodness. This purée would not taste nearly as good if the carrots were boiled and watery.*

per portion Energy 157Kcal/651kJ; Protein 4.2g; Carbohydrate 15.3g, of which sugars 13.6g; Fat 9.2g, of which saturates 1.6g; Cholesterol 1mg; Calcium 140mg; Fibre 3.3g; Sodium 78mg.

2 red (bell) peppers

1 fat aubergine (eggplant)

30–45ml/2–3 tbsp olive oil

1 red onion, cut in half lengthways and finely sliced along the grain

1 fresh red chilli, seeded and finely sliced

2 garlic cloves, chopped

5–10ml/1–2 tsp sugar

juice of 1 lemon

dash of white wine vinegar

a big handful of fresh flat leaf parsley, roughly chopped

salt and ground black pepper

lemon wedges and toasted pitta bread, to serve

SERVES 4

acvar

This is a lovely Anatolian *meze* dish of smoked aubergine and peppers with a refreshing lemony tang. Arabic in origin, it is traditionally served warm with lemon wedges to squeeze over it. Increase the quantities and serve it as a main dish with yogurt and bread, or serve it as an accompaniment to a barbecue spread.

1 Place the peppers and aubergine directly on the gas flame on top of the stove, under a conventional grill (broiler), or on a rack over the hot coals of a barbecue. Turn them from time to time until the skin is charred on all sides and the flesh feels soft. Place them in a plastic bag and leave for a few minutes.

2 One at a time, hold the charred vegetables under cold running water and peel off the skins.

3 Place them on a chopping board and remove the stalks. Halve the peppers lengthways and scoop out the seeds, then chop the flesh to a pulp. Chop the aubergine flesh to a pulp too.

4 Tip the oil into a wide, heavy pan and toss in the onion, chilli, garlic and sugar. Cook over a medium heat for 2–3 minutes, until they begin to colour.

5 Toss in the pulped peppers and aubergine, stir in the lemon juice and vinegar and season with salt and pepper. Toss in the parsley and serve with lemon wedges and toasted pitta bread.

per portion Energy 102kcal/425kJ; Protein 1.8g; Carbohydrate 10.5g, of which sugars 9.8g; Fat 6.2g, of which saturates 1g; Cholesterol 0mg; Calcium 19mg; Fibre 3.1g; Sodium 6mg.

muhammara

Made primarily of walnuts, this popular, spicy dip is usually served with toasted flat bread or chunks of crusty bread. It can also be served as a dip for raw vegetables, such as sticks of carrot and cucumber, and as an accompaniment to grilled, broiled or barbecued meats. Depending on where you are in Turkey, the ingredients may vary a little – mashed chickpeas or carrots may be used instead of bread, grated feta or yogurt may be added for a creamy texture, and garlic may be included in liberal quantities – but the general aim is to create a fiery dip spiked with Turkish red pepper or chillies. Arabic in origin, *muhammara* is traditionally made with pomegranate syrup, which actually tastes sour rather than sweet, but contemporary recipes often use lemon juice instead. The parsley leaves at the end help to cut the heat, so add more if you like.

175g/6oz/1 cup broken shelled walnuts

5ml/1 tsp cumin seeds, dry-roasted and ground

5–10ml/1–2 tsp Turkish red pepper, or 1–2 fresh red chillies, seeded and finely chopped, or 5ml/1 tsp chilli powder

1–2 garlic cloves (optional)

1 slice of day-old bread, sprinkled with water and left for a few minutes, then squeezed dry

15–30ml/1–2 tbsp tomato purée (paste)

5–10ml/1–2 tsp granulated sugar

30ml/2 tbsp pomegranate syrup or juice of 1 lemon

120ml/4fl oz/½ cup olive or sunflower oil, plus extra for serving

salt and ground black pepper

a few sprigs of fresh flat leaf parsley, to garnish

strips of pitta bread, to serve

SERVES 4–6

1 Using a mortar and pestle, pound the walnuts with the cumin seeds, red pepper or chilli and garlic (if using). Add the soaked bread and pound to a paste, then beat in the tomato purée, sugar and pomegranate syrup.

2 Now slowly drizzle in 120ml/4fl oz/ ½ cup oil, beating all the time until the paste is thick and light. Season with salt and pepper, and spoon into a bowl. Splash a little olive oil over the top to keep it moist, and garnish with parsley leaves. Serve at room temperature.

using a blender *If you have an electric blender you can make life easy and whiz all the ingredients together if you like, although many prefer the traditional mortar and pestle method as the pounding releases the natural oils and flavour of the nuts, and this contributes a lot to the finished taste.*

per portion Energy 339kcal/1399kJ; Protein 4.8g; Carbohydrate 5.1g, of which sugars 2.8g; Fat 33.4g, of which saturates 3.5g; Cholesterol 0mg; Calcium 34mg; Fibre 1.2g; Sodium 32mg.

baked chickpea purée with lemon and pine nuts

The standard chickpea purée, *humus*, found throughout the Middle East, is served as a cold *meze* dish, often with flat bread to scoop it up, or with sticks of carrot and celery for dipping into it. Thick and garlic-flavoured, it varies slightly in taste depending on whether it has sesame paste and cumin in it, but it is recognizable wherever you go. This recipe for baked *humus* is an eastern Anatolian speciality. Add yogurt to make it light, and serve it hot with warm crusty bread, pitta bread or Turkish *pide*. It is delicious served for an appetizer or light lunch with a tomato and herb salad.

225g/8oz/1¼ cups dried chickpeas, soaked in cold water for at least 6 hours or overnight

about 50ml/2fl oz/¼ cup olive oil

juice of 2 lemons

3–4 garlic cloves, crushed

10ml/2 tsp cumin seeds, crushed

30–45ml/2–3 tbsp light sesame paste (*tahin*)

45–60ml/3–4 heaped tbsp thick and creamy natural (plain) yogurt

30–45ml/2–3 tbsp pine nuts

40g/1½oz/3 tbsp butter or ghee

5–10ml/1–2 tsp oiled or roasted Turkish red pepper or paprika

salt and ground black pepper

SERVES 4

1 Drain the chickpeas, tip them into a pan and fill the pan with plenty of cold water. Bring to the boil and boil for 1 minute, then lower the heat and partially cover the pan. Simmer the chickpeas for about 1 hour, until they are soft and easy to mash. Drain, rinse well under cold running water and remove any loose skins.

2 Preheat the oven to 200°C/400°F/ Gas 6. Using a large mortar and pestle, pound the chickpeas with the oil, lemon juice, garlic and cumin. Or make life easy for yourself and whiz the ingredients in a blender.

3 Beat in the sesame paste (at this point the mixture will be very stiff), then beat in the yogurt until the purée is light and smooth. Season to taste.

4 Transfer the purée to an ovenproof dish – preferably an earthenware one – and smooth the top with the back of a spoon.

5 Dry-roast the pine nuts in a small heavy pan over a medium heat until golden brown. Lower the heat, add the butter and let it melt, then stir in the red pepper or paprika.

6 Pour the mixture over the *humus* and bake for about 25 minutes, until it has risen slightly and the butter has been absorbed. Serve straight from the oven.

sesame paste *In Turkish, sesame paste is called tahin. Greek and Middle Eastern versions, generally labelled "tahini", are available in some supermarkets and health food stores.*

per portion Energy 433kcal/1803kJ; Protein 15g; Carbohydrate 29.5g, of which sugars 3g; Fat 29.2g, of which saturates 7.7g; Cholesterol 21mg; Calcium 160mg; Fibre 6.8g; Sodium 91mg.

stir-fried spinach with currants, pine nuts and yogurt

There are endless versions of traditional spinach and yogurt *meze* dishes, ranging from plain steamed spinach served with yogurt, to this sweet and tangy Anatolian creation tamed with garlic-flavoured yogurt. Serve while still warm, with flat bread or chunks of a crusty loaf to accompany it.

350g/12oz fresh spinach leaves, thoroughly washed and drained

about 200g/7oz/scant 1 cup thick and creamy natural (plain) yogurt

2 garlic cloves, crushed

30–45ml/2–3 tbsp olive oil

1 red onion, cut in half lengthways, in half again crossways, and sliced along the grain

5ml/1 tsp sugar

15–30ml/1–2 tbsp currants, soaked in warm water for 5–10 minutes and drained

30ml/2 tbsp pine nuts

5–10ml/1–2 tsp Turkish red pepper, or 1 fresh red chilli, seeded and finely chopped

juice of 1 lemon

salt and ground black pepper

a pinch of paprika, to garnish

SERVES 3–4

1 Steam the spinach for 3–4 minutes, until wilted and soft. Drain off any excess water and chop the spinach.

2 In a bowl, beat the yogurt with the garlic. Season and set aside.

3 Heat the oil in a heavy pan and fry the onion and sugar, stirring, until the onion begins to colour. Add the currants, pine nuts and red pepper or chilli and fry until the nuts begin to colour.

4 Add the spinach, tossing it around the pan until well mixed, then pour in the lemon juice and season with salt and pepper.

5 Serve the spinach straight from the pan with the yogurt spooned on top, or tip into a serving dish and make a well in the middle, then spoon the yogurt into the well, drizzling some of it over the spinach. Serve hot, sprinkled with a little paprika.

per portion Energy 145kcal/603kJ; Protein 5.8g; Carbohydrate 10.2g, of which sugars 9.8g; Fat 9.3g, of which saturates 1.3g; Cholesterol 1mg; Calcium 252mg; Fibre 2.2g; Sodium 165mg.

bean salad with red onion, eggs, olives and anchovies

Salads made with haricot, soya, borlotti or black-eyed beans are popular as *meze* dishes, or as accompaniments to grilled, broiled or barbecued meats. Often they are simply beans, onions and flat leaf parsley tossed in olive oil, but in some homes a bean salad can be quite elaborate, served as a *meze* dish on its own or as a snack.

225g/8oz/1¼ cups dried haricot (navy), soya or black-eyed beans (peas), soaked in cold water for at least 6 hours or overnight

1 red onion, cut in half lengthways, in half again crossways, and sliced along the grain

45–60ml/3–4 tbsp black olives, drained

1 bunch of fresh flat leaf parsley, roughly chopped

60ml/4 tbsp olive oil

juice of 1 lemon

3–4 eggs, boiled until just firm, shelled and quartered

12 canned or bottled anchovy fillets, rinsed and drained

salt and ground black pepper

lemon wedges, to serve

SERVES 4

1 Drain the beans, tip them into a pan and fill the pan with plenty of cold water. Bring to the boil and boil for 1 minute, then lower the heat and partially cover the pan. Simmer the beans for about 45 minutes, until they are cooked but still firm – they should have a bite to them, and not be soft and mushy.

2 Drain the beans, rinse well under cold running water and remove any loose skins.

3 Mix the beans in a wide shallow bowl with the onion, olives and most of the parsley. Toss in the oil and lemon juice, and season with salt and pepper.

4 Place the eggs and anchovy fillets on top of the salad and sprinkle with the remaining parsley. Serve with lemon wedges for squeezing.

per portion Energy 402kcal/1674kJ; Protein 28g; Carbohydrate 10.4g, of which sugars 4.2g; Fat 28g, of which saturates 4.4g; Cholesterol 149mg; Calcium 221mg; Fibre 10g; Sodium 696mg.

2 red onions, cut in half lengthways and finely sliced along the grain

1 green (bell) pepper, seeded and finely sliced

1 fresh green chilli, seeded and chopped

2–3 garlic cloves, chopped

1 bunch of fresh flat leaf parsley, roughly chopped

225g/8oz firm feta cheese, rinsed and grated

2 large tomatoes, skinned, seeded and finely chopped

30–45ml/2–3 tbsp olive oil

salt and ground black pepper

TO SERVE

scant 5ml/1 tsp Turkish red pepper flakes or paprika

scant 5ml/1 tsp ground *sumac*

SERVES 3–4

gypsy salad with feta, chillies and parsley

There are two common salads eaten as *meze*, or served as accompaniments to meat and fish dishes. One known as *çoban salatası* or "shepherd's salad" is made of chopped cucumber, tomatoes, peppers, onion and flat leaf parsley; the other is this gypsy salad, *çingene pilavı*, meaning "gypsy rice". The mix is similar to shepherd's salad, only a chilli is included to give the desired kick, and crumbled feta is added to represent the rice.

1 Sprinkle the onions with a little salt to draw out the juice. Leave for about 10 minutes, then rinse and pat dry.

2 Put the onions and green pepper in a bowl with the chilli, garlic, parsley, feta and tomatoes.

3 Add the oil and seasoning and toss well.

4 Tip the salad into a large serving dish and sprinkle with the red pepper or paprika and *sumac*.

per portion Energy 253kcal/1049kJ; Protein 11.1g; Carbohydrate 13.4g, of which sugars 11g; Fat 17.6g, of which saturates 8.6g; Cholesterol 39mg; Calcium 260mg; Fibre 3.2g; Sodium 824mg.

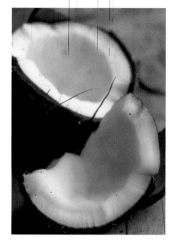

celery and coconut salad with lime

This salad is unusual for Turkey in its use of grated coconut, which is mainly reserved as a garnish for sweet dishes, or served with shelled pomegranate seeds as a medieval *meze*. Juicy and refreshing, it is welcome on a hot sunny day as part of a buffet spread outdoors, or as an accompaniment to grilled, broiled or barbecued meats and spicy dishes. It looks especially appealing served in coconut shell halves.

to make medieval *meze* *In some old-fashioned drinking haunts in Istanbul, you can still find the refreshing medieval dish of gleaming, ruby red pomegranate seeds tossed with fine shavings of fresh coconut and a squeeze of lemon or lime – a delight to the eye and very refreshing.*

45–60ml/3–4 tbsp thick and creamy natural (plain) yogurt

2 garlic cloves, crushed

5ml/1 tsp grated lime zest

juice of 1 lime

8 long celery sticks, grated (leaves reserved for the garnish)

flesh of ½ fresh coconut, grated

salt and ground black pepper

a few sprigs of fresh flat leaf parsley, to garnish

SERVES 3–4

1 Mix the yogurt and garlic in a bowl, add the lime rind and juice and season with salt and pepper.

2 Fold in the grated celery and coconut, then set aside for 15–20 minutes to let the celery juices weep. Don't leave it for too long or it will become watery.

3 To serve, spoon the salad into a bowl and garnish with celery and parsley.

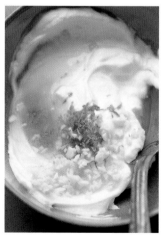

per portion Energy 126kcal/521kJ; Protein 2.1g; Carbohydrate 2.9g, of which sugars 2.9g; Fat 11.9g, of which saturates 10.1g; Cholesterol 0mg; Calcium 63mg; Fibre 3.6g; Sodium 69mg.

grated beetroot and yogurt salad

With its beneficial nutritional properties, yogurt is used frequently in *meze* dishes. It makes a tasty dip combined with mashed or grated ingredients, and mixed with a little vinegar or lemon juice it is good spooned as a sauce over grilled or fried vegetables. It is even served on its own, drizzled with a little honey, or sprinkled with icing sugar. The most famous of the yogurt dips is the one with smoked aubergine on page 24, but there are a few other gems that get little mention, such as this one made with grated beetroot. Spiked with garlic and a pretty shade of pink, it is very moreish scooped on to flat bread or chunks of a warm, crusty loaf.

4 raw beetroot (beets), washed and trimmed

500g/1¼ lb/2¼ cups thick and creamy natural (plain) yogurt

2 garlic cloves, crushed

salt and ground black pepper

a few fresh mint leaves, shredded, to garnish

SERVES 4

1 Boil the beetroot in plenty of water for 35–40 minutes until tender, but not mushy or soft. Drain and refresh under cold running water, then peel off the skins and grate the beetroot on to a plate. Squeeze it lightly with your fingers to drain off excess water.

2 In a bowl, beat the yogurt with the garlic and season with salt and pepper. Add the beetroot, reserving a little to garnish the top, and mix well. Garnish with mint leaves.

warm beetroot salad *In some households, the beetroot is diced and stir-fried with coriander seeds, sugar and a splash of apple vinegar. Then it is served warm with the cooling garlic-flavoured yogurt and garnished with dill.*

a carrot version *Cut four carrots into chunks and steam for about 15 minutes, until they are tender but still with some bite, then grate and mix with the yogurt and garlic. Season with salt and pepper and garnish with mint or dill.*

per portion Energy 95kcal/403kJ; Protein 7.8g; Carbohydrate 14.4g, of which sugars 13g; Fat 1.4g, of which saturates 0.6g; Cholesterol 2mg; Calcium 249mg; Fibre 1.3g; Sodium 137mg.

SOUPS AND HOT SNACKS

meadow yogurt soup with rice and mint

spicy red lentil soup with onion and parsley

pomegranate broth

leek soup with feta, dill and paprika

düğün çorbası

menemen

çılbır

deep-fried mussels in beer batter
with garlic-flavoured walnut sauce

filo cigars filled with feta, parsley,
mint and dill

lahmacun

Anatolian mantı

soups and hot snacks

Whether the craving is for something sweet or savoury, snacking is a vital part of Turkish daily life, with an endless variety of street stalls and cafés selling their own specialities.

Soups are linked with hot snacks in this chapter because soup is often drunk as a hot snack – both are sold at street stalls, cafés and market places, and both have a role in the home too. Soup stalls and soup houses do brisk business in every village, town and city, serving soup at all hours of the day and night. In rural Anatolia, soup is often eaten for breakfast, particularly on cold winter mornings, whereas in Istanbul late-night revellers often head to the nearest *iskembici* – the tripe soup maker. So often considered gruesome by Westerners, old favourites like sheep's head soup, sheep's trotter soup and tripe soup, with all their pungent trimmings of crushed garlic, a splash of vinegar, a bowl of pickles or a sprinkling of Turkish red pepper or chillies, are regarded by Turks as great pick-me-ups.

Although chicken and meat stocks are used to make soups, plain chicken soup itself is rare, apart from in the popular combination with noodles. *Düğün çorbası* (wedding soup) contains mutton

Above, from left to right
Çılbır, mussels, meadow yogurt soup.

or lamb, and is one of the most traditional of Turkish soups there is. It was originally known as *ekşili* (sour soup) because of its sour taste, which comes from the inclusion of lemons or vinegar. Vegetable soups, usually containing lentils or beans, are common, and almost indistinguishable from stews, apart from the fact they contain a little more liquid. Often they are so substantial that they make meals in themselves, served with chunks of crusty or flat bread. Noodle soups are also popular throughout Turkey, and in some cases resemble a liquid version of *mantı*, the Anatolian pasta parcels or dumplings served with yogurt.

In the past, soup and bread were the staple diet for soldiers, students and dervishes, so soups were made wholesome and fairly thick. The traditional method of thickening is to combine egg with lemon to make a liaison that gives the soup a sour taste, but a cheap and popular soup found in many cafés is *un çorbası* (flour soup), which is literally stock thickened with flour. It is totally uninteresting unless the stock is well-flavoured, and is generally served just as a belly-filler with croûtons or chunks of bread. Another popular and filling soup is the uniquely Anatolian *tarhana*. Made with crumbled granules of pressed, dried and fermented bulgur mixed with

yogurt and salt, it is something of an acquired taste for Westerners.

When not snacking on one of their favourite soups, Turks may well be tucking into a different kind of tasty dish, perhaps made with eggs or pastry. One of the most popular street foods is *menemen*, a combination of onions, tomatoes and peppers cooked in a pan with egg scrambled through it or cracked on top. Sold at bus and train stations, it is a good dish to eat before or after a long journey. Eggs fried with *sucuk* (spicy cured sausage) or *pastırma* (cured beef) are also popular, and other street snacks include *kokoreç* (stuffed sheep's intestines) grilled on a makeshift stove and served with half a loaf of bread, and *midye tavası* (deep-fried mussels served with a garlic-flavoured nut sauce) – a common sight along the waterfronts of Istanbul and Izmir.

Anatolian hot snacks consist of the famous *lahmacun*, a pizza-like flat bread topped with minced (ground) meat, parsley and lemon, and a number of *mantı* dishes (a cross between noodles and dumplings). In Istanbul, the Ottomans left a legacy of savoury pastries – during the reign of Sultan Mehmet IV, the Palace pastry chefs took their role very seriously, and the city's pastry cooks had to adhere to their recipes and methods or risk being punished.

There are about a dozen different types of savoury pastries (*börek*), their fillings varying according to the region they come from. The most common fillings found throughout Turkey include mashed white cheese with herbs, spinach and onions, and one made with finely minced lamb or beef and onions. Regional specialities can also include puréed pumpkin or potato, baked aubergine (eggplant) and cheese, and fish with herbs. Doughs vary from the most ancient form of flat bread (the traditional *yufka* rounds), for which filo can be substituted, to more complex doughs that are similar to Western flaky and puff pastries. *Su böreği* forms a link between pastry and dough – sheets of boiled pastry and filling layered and baked in the same way as Italian lasagne.

Having travelled the silk trade routes from China to eastern Anatolia, *mantı* is the most ancient form of pasta. As many of the migrating Turks settled in the fertile plains around Kayseri, this central region has become known for its *mantı* makers. Traditionally, the noodle dough is stuffed with seasoned minced lamb or beef, baked in the oven, and served with garlic-flavoured yogurt and a little melted butter or ghee. Modern versions often omit the butter and spoon a fresh tomato sauce over boiled, plain noodle dumplings.

Above, from left to right
Leek soup with feta, spicy lentil soup, menemen.

meadow yogurt soup with rice and mint

In every soup house, bus station and roadside café throughout Turkey you will come across yogurt soup. Based on well-flavoured stock and yogurt, it usually contains a little rice, bulgur, chickpeas or barley, depending on which region you are in, and occasionally it is coloured with saffron or sprinkled with paprika. When it is flavoured with dried mint, it is called *yayla çorbası*, or meadow soup. Chunks of crusty bread are the best accompaniment.

15ml/1 tbsp butter or sunflower oil

1 large onion, finely chopped

scant 15ml/1 tbsp plain (all-purpose) flour

1.2 litres/2 pints/5 cups lamb or chicken stock

75g/3oz/scant ½ cup long grain rice (wild or plain), well rinsed

15–30ml/1–2 tbsp dried mint

400ml/14fl oz/1²⁄₃ cups thick and creamy natural (plain) yogurt, strained (see below)

salt and ground black pepper

SERVES 4

1 Melt the butter in a heavy pan, add the onion and cook until soft. Take the pan off the heat and stir in the flour, then pour in the stock, stirring all the time. Return the pan to the heat and bring the stock to the boil, stirring often.

2 Stir in the rice and most of the mint, reserving a little for the garnish. Lower the heat, cover the pan and simmer for about 20 minutes, until the rice is cooked. Season with salt and pepper.

3 Beat the yogurt until smooth, then spoon almost all of it into the soup. Keep the heat low and stir vigorously to make sure the yogurt remains smooth and creamy and becomes well blended. Ladle the soup into bowls, swirl in the remaining yogurt, and garnish with the remaining mint.

straining yogurt *If you can't get strained yogurt you can make it yourself. Line a sieve (strainer) with a piece of muslin (cheesecloth) and spoon thick and creamy plain yogurt into it. Allow the excess liquid to drip through the muslin, then tip the strained yogurt from the sieve into a bowl.*

per portion Energy 187kcal/781kJ; Protein 7.6g; Carbohydrate 30.3g, of which sugars 11.1g; Fat 4.4g, of which saturates 2.5g; Cholesterol 9mg; Calcium 215mg; Fibre 1g; Sodium 108mg.

spicy red lentil soup
with onion and parsley

In Istanbul and Izmir, lentil soups are light and subtly spiced, and served as an appetizer or as a snack. In Anatolia, lentil and bean soups are made with chunks of mutton and flavoured with tomato and spices, and are usually served as a meal on their own.

30–45ml/2–3 tbsp olive or sunflower oil

1 large onion, finely chopped

2 garlic cloves, finely chopped

1 fresh red chilli, seeded and finely chopped

5–10ml/1–2 tsp cumin seeds

5–10ml/1–2 tsp coriander seeds

1 carrot, finely chopped

scant 5ml/1 tsp ground fenugreek

5ml/1 tsp sugar

15ml/1 tbsp tomato purée (paste)

250g/9oz/generous 1 cup split red lentils

1.75 litres/3 pints/7½ cups chicken stock

salt and ground black pepper

TO SERVE

1 small red onion, finely chopped

1 large bunch of fresh flat leaf parsley, finely chopped

4–6 lemon wedges

SERVES 4–6

1 Heat the oil in a heavy pan and stir in the onion, garlic, chilli, cumin and coriander seeds. When the onion begins to colour, toss in the carrot and cook for 2–3 minutes. Add the fenugreek, sugar and tomato purée and stir in the lentils.

2 Pour in the stock, stir well and bring to the boil. Lower the heat, partially cover the pan and simmer for 30–40 minutes, until the lentils have broken up.

3 If the soup is too thick, thin it down with a little water. Season with salt and pepper to taste.

4 Serve the soup straight from the pan or, if you prefer a smooth texture, whiz it in a blender, then reheat if necessary. Ladle the soup into bowls and sprinkle liberally with the chopped onion and parsley. Serve with a wedge of lemon to squeeze over the soup.

per portion Energy 203kcal/856kJ; Protein 11.1g; Carbohydrate 31.8g, of which sugars 7.3g; Fat 4.4g, of which saturates 0.6g; Cholesterol 0mg; Calcium 45mg; Fibre 3.5g; Sodium 26mg.

pomegranate broth

With its origins in Persia and Azerbaijan, this fresh-tasting delicate soup, *narlı çorba*, is perhaps the best way of appreciating sour pomegranates, as it is both pleasing to the eye and the palate. Clear and refreshing, it is served as a sophisticated palate cleanser between courses, or as a light appetizer to a meal. Sour pomegranates are available in Middle Eastern stores, but if you can only find sweet pomegranates, use them with the juice of a lemon.

1.2 litres/2 pints/5 cups clear chicken stock

150ml/¼ pint/⅔ cup sour pomegranate juice (see below)

seeds of 1 sweet pomegranate

salt and ground black pepper

fresh mint leaves, to garnish

SERVES 4

1 Pour the stock into a pan and bring to the boil. Lower the heat, stir in the pomegranate juice, and lemon juice if using sweet pomegranates, then bring the stock back to the boil.

2 Lower the heat again and stir in half the pomegranate seeds, then season and turn off the heat.

3 Ladle the hot broth into warmed bowls. Sprinkle the remaining pomegranate seeds over the top and garnish with mint leaves.

pomegranates *A fruit from antiquity, the pomegranate has symbolized beauty, fertility and prosperity and, according to the medieval Islamic mystics, it purged the soul of anger and envy. Cultivated in the Middle East, it has long been used in the cooking of this region, and is also thought by some to have magical properties. The ruby-red grains of sweet pomegranates are eaten fresh, whereas the sour fruits are used in soups, marinades, dressings and syrups, and to make a cooling sherbet drink.*

extracting pomegranate juice *For 150ml/¼ pint/⅔ cup juice, you will need 5–6 sour pomegranates. Cut the pomegranates in half crossways and squeeze them with a stainless-steel, glass or wooden lemon squeezer to extract the juice. Do not use any metal other than stainless-steel for squeezing or it will react with the astringent juice of the pomegranates, causing the juice to discolour and taste unpleasant.*

per portion Energy 62kcal/260kJ; Protein 2g; Carbohydrate 3.9g, of which sugars 2.3g; Fat 4.4g, of which saturates 0.4g; Cholesterol 0mg; Calcium 14mg; Fibre 0.6g; Sodium 205mg.

leek soup with feta, dill and paprika

Creamy leek soup is a popular home-cooked dish in Turkey. Flavoured with dill and topped with crumbled white cheese, this one is warming and satisfying. The saltiness of feta is good in this soup, but you could just as well use Roquefort or Parmesan, both of which are equally salty, and you could substitute croûtons for the cheese. Serve with chunks of fresh, crusty bread.

30ml/2 tbsp olive or sunflower oil

3 leeks, trimmed, roughly chopped and washed

1 onion, chopped

5ml/1 tsp sugar

1 bunch of fresh dill, chopped, with a few fronds reserved for the garnish

300ml/½ pint/1¼ cups milk

15ml/1 tbsp butter (optional)

115g/4oz feta cheese, crumbled

salt and ground black pepper

paprika, to garnish

SERVES 3–4

1 Heat the oil in a heavy pan and stir in the chopped leeks and onion. Cook for about 10 minutes, or until the vegetables are soft.

2 Add the sugar and chopped dill, and pour in 600ml/1 pint/2½ cups water. Bring to the boil, lower the heat and simmer for about 15 minutes.

3 Leave the liquid to cool a little, then process in a blender until smooth.

4 Return the puréed soup to the pan, pour in the milk and stir over a gentle heat until it is hot (don't let it come to the boil).

5 Season with salt and pepper, bearing in mind that the feta is salty. If using the butter, drop it onto the surface of the soup and let it melt.

6 Ladle the soup into bowls and top with the crumbled feta. Serve immediately, garnished with a little paprika and the dill fronds.

per portion Energy 203kcal/844kJ; Protein 10g; Carbohydrate 10.9g, of which sugars 9.4g; Fat 13.5g, of which saturates 5.7g; Cholesterol 25mg; Calcium 259mg; Fibre 4.1g; Sodium 454mg.

500g/1¼lb lamb on the bone – neck, leg or shoulder

2 carrots, roughly chopped

2 potatoes, roughly chopped

1 cinnamon stick

45ml/3 tbsp strained (natural) plain yogurt

45ml/3 tbsp plain (all-purpose) flour

1 egg yolk

juice of ½ lemon

30ml/2 tbsp butter

5ml/1 tsp Turkish red pepper or paprika

salt and ground black pepper

SERVES 4–6

düğün çorbası

This is the soup of Turkish weddings. Steeped in tradition, it varies little throughout the country, the only difference being the inclusion of cinnamon to flavour the stock. Made with lamb stock and containing chunks of cooked lamb, it is slightly sour from the classic liaison of lemon, egg and yogurt.

1 Place the lamb in a deep pan with the carrots, potatoes and cinnamon. Pour in 2 litres/3½ pints/8 cups water and bring to the boil, then skim any scum off the surface and lower the heat.

2 Cover and simmer for about 1½ hours, until the meat is so tender that it almost falls off the bone. Lift the lamb out of the pan and place it on a chopping board.

3 Remove the meat from the bone and chop it into small pieces. Strain the stock and discard the carrots and potatoes. Pour the stock back into the pan, season and bring to the boil.

4 In a deep bowl, beat the yogurt with the flour. Add the egg yolk and lemon juice and beat well again, then pour in about 250ml/8fl oz/1 cup of the hot stock, beating all the time.

5 Lower the heat under the pan and pour the yogurt mixture into the stock, beating constantly. Add the meat and heat through.

6 Melt the butter in a small pan and stir in the red pepper or paprika.

7 Ladle the soup into bowls and drizzle the pepper butter over the top.

per portion Energy 226kcal/943kJ; Protein 15g; Carbohydrate 14.4g, of which sugars 3.6g; Fat 12.4g, of which saturates 6.2g; Cholesterol 88mg; Calcium 54mg; Fibre 1.4g; Sodium 87mg.

menemen

This is Turkish street food. Cooked on makeshift stoves at bus and train stations, ports and rest houses, it is a satisfying snack or meal. Depending on the cook, the eggs are either stirred into the tomato and pepper ragoût to scramble them, or they are cracked on top and cooked in the steam of a domed lid until just set.

15ml/1 tbsp olive oil

15ml/1 tbsp butter

2 red onions, cut in half lengthways and sliced along the grain

1 red or green (bell) pepper, halved lengthways, seeded and sliced

2 garlic cloves, roughly chopped

5–10ml/1–2 tsp Turkish red pepper, or 1 fresh red chilli, seeded and sliced

400g/14oz can chopped tomatoes

5–10ml/1–2 tsp sugar

4 eggs

salt and ground black pepper

TO SERVE

90ml/6 tbsp thick and creamy natural (plain) yogurt

1–2 garlic cloves, crushed

a handful of fresh flat leaf parsley, roughly chopped

SERVES 4

1 Heat the oil and butter in a heavy frying pan. Stir in the onions, sliced pepper, garlic and Turkish red pepper or chilli and cook until they begin to soften.

2 Add the tomatoes and sugar and mix them in well. Cook for about 10 minutes, or until the liquid has reduced and the mixture is quite saucy, then season with salt and pepper.

3 Crack the eggs over the top of the tomato mixture, cover the pan and cook until the eggs are just done.

4 Meanwhile, beat the yogurt with the garlic in a bowl and season with salt and pepper.

5 Ladle the soup into bowls and serve hot, topped with parsley and dollops of garlic-flavoured yogurt.

individual servings *If you like, you can divide the tomato mixture between four small pans and crack an egg into each one so that each person has their own serving.*

per portion Energy 190kcal/790kJ; Protein 8.6g; Carbohydrate 14.9g, of which sugars 12.4g; Fat 11.2g, of which saturates 3.5g; Cholesterol 196mg; Calcium 65mg; Fibre 3.1g; Sodium 101mg.

500g/1¼lb/2¼ cups thick and
natural (plain) yogurt

2 garlic cloves, crushed

30–45ml/2–3 tbsp white wine vinegar

4 large (US extra large) eggs

15–30ml/1–2 tbsp butter

5ml/1 tsp Turkish red pepper or paprika

a few dried sage leaves, crumbled

salt and ground black pepper

SERVES 2

other egg variations *Popular egg
recipes include* yumurtali ispanak kavurmasi,
*a dish of sautéed spinach and onions with
an egg cooked in the middle, and a classic
Palace dish of eggs cooked with* pastırma.

çılbır

This dish of poached eggs on a bed of garlic-flavoured yogurt is
surprisingly delicious. In Turkey it is served as a hot *meze* dish or
snack, but it works equally well as a supper dish with a green salad.
Hen's eggs or duck's eggs can be used, whichever you prefer, and
you can either poach or fry them. Spiked with Turkish red pepper or
paprika, and served with toasted flat bread or chunks of a warm,
crispy loaf, it is simple and satisfying.

1 Beat the yogurt with the garlic and
seasoning. Spoon into a serving dish or
on to individual plates, spreading it flat
to create a thick mattress for the eggs.
Serve at room temperature as a contrast
to the hot eggs, or heat it by placing the
dish in a cooling oven, or by sitting it in
a covered pan of hot water.

2 Fill a pan with water, add the
vinegar to seal the egg whites, and bring
to a rolling boil. Stir the water with a
spoon to create a whirlpool and crack in
the first egg. As the egg spins and the
white sets around the yolk, stir the water
for the next one. Poach each egg for 2–3
minutes so the yolk is still soft.

3 Lift the eggs out of the water with a
slotted spoon and place them on the
yogurt mattress.

4 Quickly melt the butter in a small
pan. Stir in the red pepper or paprika
and sage leaves, then spoon over the
eggs. Eat immediately.

per portion Energy 345kcal/1438kJ; Protein 25.4g; Carbohydrate 19.1g, of which sugars 19.1g; Fat 19.8g, of which saturates 8.3g; Cholesterol 400mg; Calcium 534mg; Fibre 0.1g; Sodium 393mg.

deep-fried mussels in beer batter with garlic-flavoured walnut sauce

Fried in huge, curved pans, *midye tavası* are skewered on sticks and sold in batches, with a garlic-flavoured *tarator* sauce that can be made with pounded walnuts, almonds or pine nuts, or simply with day-old bread. A speciality from Istanbul and Izmir, they are very much part of the street-food scene, as well as one of the popular hot *meze* dishes in fish restaurants.

sunflower oil, for deep-frying

about 50 fresh mussels, cleaned, shelled and patted dry (see below)

FOR THE BATTER

115g/4oz/1 cup plain (all-purpose) flour

5ml/1 tsp salt

2.5ml/½ tsp bicarbonate of soda (baking soda)

2 egg yolks

175–250ml/6–8fl oz/¾–1 cup beer or lager

FOR THE SAUCE

75g/3oz/½ cup broken shelled walnuts

2 slices of day-old bread, sprinkled with water and left for a few minutes, then squeezed dry

2–3 garlic cloves, crushed

45–60ml/3–4 tbsp olive oil

juice of 1 lemon

dash of white wine vinegar

salt and ground black pepper

SERVES 4–5

1 Make the batter. Sift the flour, salt and soda into a bowl. Make a well in the middle and drop in the egg yolks. Using a wooden spoon, slowly beat in the beer and draw in the flour from the sides of the well until a smooth, thick batter is formed. Set aside for 30 minutes.

2 Meanwhile, make the sauce. Pound the walnuts to a paste using a mortar and pestle, or whiz them in a blender. Add the bread and garlic, and pound again to a paste. Drizzle in the olive oil, stirring all the time, and beat in the lemon juice and vinegar. The sauce should be smooth, with the consistency of thick double (heavy) cream – if it is too dry, stir in a little water. Season with salt and pepper and set aside.

3 Heat enough sunflower oil for deep-frying in a wok or other deep-sided pan. Using your fingers, dip each mussel into the batter and drop into the hot oil. Fry in batches for a minute or two until golden brown. Lift out with a slotted spoon and drain on kitchen paper.

4 Thread the mussels on wooden skewers, or spear them individually, and serve hot, accompanied by the garlic-flavoured dipping sauce.

preparing the mussels *Raw mussels are prised from their shells with ease by the street vendors, but you may find the job too fiddly. An easier option is to steam them open for 3–4 minutes, then remove them from their shells, or use the ready-shelled mussels sold frozen in bags.*

per portion Energy 439kcal/1827kJ; Protein 10.6g; Carbohydrate 24.6g, of which sugars 1.9g; Fat 33g, of which saturates 4g; Cholesterol 89mg; Calcium 115mg; Fibre 1.5g; Sodium 502mg.

filo cigars filled with feta, parsley, mint and dill

These classic cigar-shaped pastries, *sigara böreği*, are popular snack and *meze* food, and they are also good as nibbles with drinks. Here they are filled them with cheese and herbs, but other popular fillings include aromatic minced meat, baked aubergine and cheese, or mashed pumpkin, cheese and dill. The filo pastry can be folded into triangles, but cigars are the most traditional shape. They can be prepared in advance and kept under a damp dish towel in the refrigerator until you are ready to fry them.

making a puff pastry log *Use the same filling for a pastry log,* kol böreği. *Roll out a 400g/14oz packet puff pastry and spoon on the filling. Roll into a log, tucking in the ends as you go, and place on an oiled baking tray. Cut diagonally into portions, keeping it intact at the base. Brush with a mixture of egg yolk and sunflower oil and bake in a preheated oven at 180°C/350°F/ Gas 4 for 30 minutes, or until crisp. Cut into portions as soon as it is out of the oven.*

225g/8oz feta cheese

1 large (US extra large) egg, lightly beaten

1 small bunch each of fresh flat leaf parsley, mint and dill, finely chopped

4–5 sheets of filo pastry

sunflower oil, for deep-frying

dill fronds, to garnish (optional)

SERVES 3–4

1 In a bowl, mash the feta with a fork. Beat in the egg and fold in the herbs.

2 Place the sheets of filo on a flat surface and cover with a damp dish towel to keep them moist. Working with one sheet at a time, cut the filo into strips about 10–13cm/4–5in wide, and pile them on top of each other. Keep the strips covered with another damp dish towel.

3 Lay one filo strip on the surface in front of you and place a heaped teaspoon of the cheese filling along one of the short ends. Roll the end over the filling, quite tightly to keep it in place, then tuck in the sides to seal in the filling and continue to roll until you get to the other end.

4 As you reach the end, brush the tip with a little water – this will help seal the filo and prevent it unravelling during cooking. Place the filled cigar, join-side down, on a plate and cover with another damp dish towel to keep it moist. Continue with the remaining sheets of filo and filling.

5 Heat enough oil for deep-frying in a wok or other deep-sided pan, and deep-fry the filo cigars in batches for 5–6 minutes until crisp and golden brown. Lift out of the oil with a slotted spoon and drain on kitchen paper.

6 Serve immediately, garnished with dill fronds if you like.

per portion Energy 311Kcal/1291kJ; Protein 12.4g; Carbohydrate 11.2g, of which sugars 1.6g; Fat 24.4g, of which saturates 9.5g; Cholesterol 92mg; Calcium 278mg; Fibre 1.6g; Sodium 838mg.

lahmacun

This Anatolian snack is a great culinary creation. The thin crispy base is smeared with a layer of lightly spiced lamb and rolled into a cone with fresh parsley, *sumac* and a squeeze of lemon.

scant 5ml/1 tsp active dried yeast

2.5ml/½ tsp sugar

150ml/¼ pint/⅔ cup lukewarm water

350g/12oz/3 cups strong white bread flour

2.5ml/½ tsp salt

a few drops of sunflower oil

FOR THE TOPPING

15ml/1 tbsp olive oil

15ml/1 tbsp butter

1 onion, finely chopped

2 garlic cloves, finely chopped

225g/8oz/1 cup finely minced (ground) lean lamb

30ml/2 tbsp tomato purée (paste)

15ml/1 tbsp sugar

5–10ml/1–2 tsp Turkish red pepper, or 1 fresh red chilli, finely chopped

5ml/1 tsp dried mint

5–10ml/1–2 tsp ground *sumac*

1 bunch of fresh flat leaf parsley, roughly chopped

1 lemon, halved

salt and ground black pepper

SERVES 2–4

1 Make the dough. Put the yeast and sugar into a small bowl with half the lukewarm water. Set aside for about 15 minutes until frothy.

2 Sift the flour and salt into a large bowl, make a well in the middle and add the creamed yeast and the rest of the lukewarm water. Using your hand, draw in the flour and work the mixture to a dough, adding more water if necessary.

3 Turn the dough on to a lightly floured surface and knead until it is smooth and elastic. Drip a few drops of sunflower oil into the base of the bowl and roll the dough in it. Cover the bowl with a damp dish towel and leave in a warm place for about 1 hour or until the dough has doubled in size.

4 Meanwhile, prepare the topping. Heat the oil and butter in a heavy pan and gently fry the onion and garlic until they soften. Leave to cool in the pan.

5 Put the lamb in a bowl, add the tomato purée, sugar, red pepper or chilli and mint, then the softened onion and garlic. Season with salt and pepper, and mix and knead with your hands. Cover and keep in the refrigerator until you are ready to use.

6 Place two baking sheets in the oven. Preheat the oven to 220°C/425°F/Gas 7.

7 Punch down the risen dough, knead it on a lightly floured surface, then divide into 2 or 4 equal pieces. Roll each piece into a thin flat round, stretching the dough with your hands as you roll.

8 Oil the hot baking sheets and place the rounds on them, then cover with a thin layer of meat mixture, spreading it right to the edges. Bake for 15–20 minutes, until the meat is nicely cooked.

9 As soon as the *lahmacun* are ready, sprinkle them with the *sumac* and parsley. Squeeze a little lemon juice over the top and roll them up while the dough is still pliable. Eat like a pizza – with your hands, or on plates with a knife and fork.

per portion Energy 496kcal/2092kJ; Protein 20g; Carbohydrate 75.2g, of which sugars 8.1g; Fat 14.9g, of which saturates 6.1g; Cholesterol 51mg; Calcium 167mg; Fibre 3.8g; Sodium 333mg.

Anatolian mantı

Falling between a Chinese dumpling and Italian pasta, baked *mantı* is a popular snack in eastern Anatolia. The chickpea filling is good for vegetarians. Serve as a hot snack, or as a meal on its own.

450g/1lb/4 cups plain (all-purpose) flour

2.5ml/½ tsp salt

1 whole egg, beaten with 1 egg yolk

salt and ground black pepper

FOR THE FILLING

400g/14oz can chickpeas, drained and thoroughly rinsed

5ml/1 tsp cumin seeds, crushed

5ml/1 tsp Turkish red pepper or paprika

FOR THE YOGURT

about 90ml/6 tbsp thick and creamy natural (plain) yogurt

2–3 garlic cloves, crushed

FOR THE SAUCE

15ml/1 tbsp olive oil

15ml/1 tbsp butter

1 onion, finely chopped

2 garlic cloves, finely chopped

5ml/1 tsp Turkish red pepper, or 1 fresh red chilli, seeded and finely chopped

5–10ml/1–2 tsp granulated sugar

5–10ml/1–2 tsp dried mint

400g/14oz can chopped tomatoes, drained of juice

600ml/1 pint/2½ cups vegetable or chicken stock

1 small bunch each of fresh flat leaf parsley and coriander (cilantro), roughly chopped

SERVES 4–6

1 Make the dough. Sift the flour and salt into a wide bowl and make a well in the middle. Pour in the beaten egg and 50ml/2fl oz/¼ cup water. Using your fingers, draw the flour into the liquid and mix to a dough.

2 Knead the dough for 10 minutes, cover the bowl with a damp dish towel and leave the dough to rest for 1 hour.

3 Meanwhile, prepare the filling and yogurt. In a bowl, mash the chickpeas with a fork. Beat in the cumin, red pepper or paprika and seasoning. In another bowl, beat the yogurt with the garlic and season with salt and pepper.

4 Make the sauce. Heat the oil and butter in a heavy pan and gently fry the onion and garlic until softened. Add the red pepper or chilli, sugar and mint, then stir in the tomatoes and cook gently for about 15 minutes, until the sauce is thick. Season and remove from the heat.

5 Preheat the oven to 200°C/400°F/ Gas 6. Roll out the dough as thinly as possible on a lightly floured surface. Using a sharp knife, cut the dough into small squares (roughly 2.5cm/1in).

6 Spoon a little chickpea mixture into the middle of each square and bunch the corners together to form a little pouch. Place the filled pasta parcels in a greased ovenproof dish, stacking them next to each other. Bake, uncovered, for 15–20 minutes, until golden brown.

7 Pour the stock into a pan and bring to the boil. Take the pasta parcels out of the oven and pour the stock over them.

8 Return the dish to the oven and bake for a further 15–20 minutes, until almost all the stock has been absorbed. Meanwhile, reheat the tomato sauce.

9 Transfer to a serving dish and spoon the yogurt over them. Top the cool yogurt with the hot tomato sauce and sprinkle with the chopped herbs.

per portion Energy 416kcal/1760kJ; Protein 14.8g; Carbohydrate 73.7g, of which sugars 5.9g; Fat 9g, of which saturates 2.6g; Cholesterol 71mg; Calcium 179mg; Fibre 5.9g; Sodium 360mg.

VEGETARIAN AND VEGETABLE DISHES

ımam bayıldı

smoked aubergines in cheese sauce

green beans with tomatoes and dill

caramelized mushrooms with allspice
and herbs

artichokes with beans and almonds

carrot and apricot rolls with mint yogurt

potatoes baked with tomatoes, olives,
feta and oregano

kabak mucver

roasted courgettes and peaches with
pine nuts

elma dolması

vegetarian and vegetable dishes

Bought daily, vegetables are cooked in simple and versatile dishes that can be served as *meze*, with rice or meat, or on their own with a squeeze of lemon and some creamy yogurt.

Turkish vegetable cuisine follows the natural cycle of seasonal produce. Everyone talks about the dishes they are going to cook as each season brings on its speciality. From early winter to spring the kitchens in the south of Turkey are graced with long and elegant, bright purple carrots, grated for salads or cooked with nuts to make *cezerye*, a special *helva* from Gaziantep, while the kitchens in the north are filled with the sweet aroma of pumpkin cubes poaching in syrup to make the delectable dessert, *bal kabağı tatlısı*. Early summer is the season for young, crisp, marble-white courgettes (zucchini), often topped with their yellow flowers, and all summer long the most loved of all vegetables, the aubergine or eggplant, is cooked in a myriad creative ways.

Visiting the market is very much part of the day's activities in most Turkish homes. Choosing the vegetables for lunch or supper can be quite

Above, from left to right
Parmesan cheese,
caramelized mushrooms,
pine nuts.

time-consuming, but the cooks have lots of fun picking over the vegetables on display and haggling with the sellers. Often the selection of vegetables on offer will dictate the meals of the day – there might be fresh broad (fava) beans bursting from their pods, or regal-looking young globe artichokes artfully prepared for cooking – all so tempting and too good to miss. Cucumbers are often peeled at the market and sold as a refreshing snack, or taken home and cut into strips then lightly salted to serve as a nibble with a drink. Similarly, giant cos lettuces are taken home and placed in a jug (pitcher) of water on the table for everyone to help themselves to a crunchy leaf and sprinkle it with a little salt.

All vegetables are eaten fresh in season, and some are preserved in pickles and jams. The unique vegetable jams, such as the ones made with firm plum tomatoes or whole baby aubergines, are enjoyed in Anatolia with bread, as well as with white cheese as a snack. Vegetables are generally tossed into salads, or cooked in olive oil and eaten cold. They are also stuffed and baked, and grilled (broiled), roasted or fried. When aubergines, courgettes and *çarliston biber* (sweet green peppers shaped like Turkish slippers) are fried, they are traditionally served with a sauce, such as yogurt mixed with garlic and a

dash of vinegar. And the elegant *zeytinyağlı* dishes, which are a legacy of the Palace kitchens, in which the vegetables are cooked in olive oil and served at room temperature so the flavoured oil becomes part of the dish, are a particular favourite in Istanbul.

Dolma is Turkish for stuffed vegetables. In fact, it is the word used for anything that is stuffed, even *dolmuş* a taxi stuffed with people. If there is no natural cavity to stuff, the Turks will create one. Take the aubergine, for example. After a great deal of expert bashing and massaging, and without splitting it open, the innards spit out through a hole at one end so the skin can be stuffed. Fruit, such as apples, plums and prunes, are also used for stuffing, and cabbage and vine leaves are wrapped around rice fillings to make log-shaped *dolma*. One of the most popular fillings is the vegetarian aromatic rice with pine nuts, currants and herbs, but vegetables may also be stuffed with meat and rice.

Vegetables play an important role in the culinary culture of the Turks, who have a pathological fascination for the health properties of the food they eat. It is not unusual to find baskets of dried medicinal herbs and vegetables, as well as their seeds and roots, alongside piles of fresh vegetables in the markets. Aubergines are believed to be beneficial for infections of the ovaries, courgettes for intestinal parasites, onions for ulcers, cabbage for stomach pains, garlic for blood circulation and overall good health – and so on. Throughout the Seljuk and Ottoman periods, many recipes were based on the ancient Chinese theory of Yin and Yang, that some vegetables warm the blood, while others cool it. As a result, Turkish cuisine is blessed with lots of healthy vegetable food, many of which are found in the broad spectrum of *meze*, salads and vegetarian dishes.

Purple carrots; red onions; twisted hot green peppers; aubergines shaped like boxer's gloves or slender ones the length of a forearm; ripe tomatoes; large, reddish-green, crisp apples and perfumed quince; stacks of fresh vine leaves; baskets of long-stemmed herbs; huge marrows (large zucchini) and pumpkins; white and green courgettes with their pretty yellow flowers; long fingers of okra; giant cabbages like tortoises; leeks the size of baseball bats – the Turkish markets are colourful and brimming with fresh fruit and vegetables. Brought in daily from the fertile plains, this wonderfully fresh produce is ready to be stuffed, poached, baked, smoked, cooked in meat stews or vegetarian casseroles, or destined for the Palace *zeytinyağlı* dishes.

Above, from left to right
Aubergine (eggplant), artichokes with beans and almonds, courgettes (zucchini).

ımam bayıldı

Whether the Imam fainted from shock or pleasure at the quantity of olive oil used in this dish, no one knows, but "the Imam fainted" is the translation of *ımam bayıldı*. The aubergines are sometimes baked, but the more traditional method is gentle poaching on top of the stove – when cooked this way they melt in the mouth. Serve as a *meze* dish or with a green salad for lunch or supper.

2 good-sized aubergines (eggplants)

sunflower oil, for shallow frying

1 bunch each of fresh flat leaf parsley and dill

1 large onion, halved and finely sliced

3 tomatoes, skinned and finely chopped

2–3 garlic cloves, finely chopped

5ml/1 tsp salt

150ml/¼ pint/⅔ cup olive oil

juice of ½ lemon

15ml/1 tbsp sugar

lemon wedges, to serve

SERVES 4

1 Using a vegetable peeler or a small, sharp knife, peel the aubergines lengthways in stripes like a zebra. Place them in a bowl of salted water for 5 minutes, then drain and pat dry.

2 Heat about 1cm/½in sunflower oil in a wok or deep-sided pan. Place the aubergines in the oil and fry quickly on all sides to soften them. This should take a total of 3–5 minutes.

3 Lift the aubergines out on to a chopping board and slit them open lengthways to create pockets, keeping the bottoms and both ends intact so they look like canoes when stuffed.

4 Reserve a few dill fronds and parsley leaves for the garnish, then chop the rest and mix them in a bowl with the onion, tomatoes and garlic. Add the salt and a little of the olive oil.

5 Spoon the mixture into the aubergine pockets, packing it in tightly so that all of it is used up.

6 Place the filled aubergines side by side in a deep, heavy pan. Mix the remaining olive oil with 50ml/2fl oz/ ¼ cup water and the lemon juice, pour it over the aubergines, and sprinkle the sugar over the top.

7 Cover the pan with its lid and place over a medium heat to get the oil hot and create some steam. Lower the heat and cook the aubergines very gently for about 1 hour, basting from time to time. They should be soft and tender, with only a little oil left in the bottom of the pan.

8 Leave the aubergines to cool in the pan, then carefully transfer them to a serving dish and spoon the oil from the bottom of the pan over them. Garnish with the reserved dill and parsley and serve at room temperature, with lemon wedges for squeezing.

a baked variation *Follow steps 1–5, then place the filled aubergines in an ovenproof dish. Drizzle the remaining olive oil and lemon juice over the top, cover with foil and bake for about 45 minutes at 180°C/350°F/Gas 4. Remove the foil, sprinkle a little grated Parmesan cheese over the top and return the aubergines to the oven for about 15 minutes, until nicely browned. Serve hot.*

per portion Energy 407kcal/1680kJ; Protein 3g; Carbohydrate 16.7g, of which sugars 14.1g; Fat 37g, of which saturates 5.1g; Cholesterol 0mg; Calcium 67mg; Fibre 4.8g; Sodium 507mg.

smoked aubergines in cheese sauce

This recipe is adapted from the traditional Palace dish, *Hünkar beğendi*, which was created for one of the Ottoman sultans. Invariably, the dish consists of lamb and tomato stew, or meatballs cooked in a tomato sauce, served on a bed of aubergine in a cheese sauce. Here, the *beğendi* is baked in the oven and served on its own – a warming and nourishing dish that is popular with children. Serve it as a main dish for lunch or supper with chunks of fresh, crusty bread and a juicy green salad.

2 large aubergines (eggplants)

50g/2oz/¼ cup butter

30ml/2 tbsp plain (all-purpose) flour

600ml/1 pint/2½ cups milk (you may need a little more)

115g/4oz Cheddar cheese, grated

salt and ground black pepper

finely grated Parmesan cheese, for the topping

SERVES 4

1 Preheat the oven to 200°C/400°F/ Gas 6. Put the aubergines directly on the gas flame on top of the stove, or under a conventional grill (broiler), and turn them until the skin is charred on all sides and the flesh feels soft. Place in a plastic bag and leave for a few minutes.

2 Hold each aubergine by the stalk under cold running water and gently peel off the charred skin.

3 Squeeze the flesh with your fingers to get rid of any excess water and place on a chopping board. Remove the stalks and chop the flesh to a pulp.

4 Make the sauce. Melt the butter in a heavy pan, remove from the heat and stir in the flour. Slowly beat in the milk, then return the pan to a medium heat and cook, stirring constantly, until the sauce is smooth and thick.

5 Beat in the grated Cheddar cheese a little at a time, then beat in the aubergine pulp and season with salt and pepper.

6 Tip the mixture into a baking dish and sprinkle a generous layer of Parmesan over the top.

7 Bake in the oven for about 25 minutes, until the top is nicely browned.

per portion Energy 322kcal/1344kJ; Protein 14.1g; Carbohydrate 15.2g, of which sugars 9.3g; Fat 22.7g, of which saturates 14.5g; Cholesterol 63mg; Calcium 415mg; Fibre 2.2g; Sodium 350mg.

1–2 onions, roughly chopped

2 garlic cloves, roughly chopped

30–45ml/2–3 tbsp olive oil

500g/1¼lb stringless runner
(green) beans, trimmed and each
cut into 3–4 pieces

15ml/1 tbsp sugar

juice of 1 lemon

2 x 400g/14oz cans chopped tomatoes

a handful of fresh dill, roughly chopped

salt and ground pepper

SERVES 4 (AS A MAIN DISH)

green beans with
tomatoes and dill

This is a delicious "olive oil" dish. As part of a *meze* spread it is
served at room temperature, but in a Turkish home it may be
served hot as a side dish to accompany grilled, broiled or barbecued
poultry and meat, or as a main course with a dollop of creamy
yogurt. When runner beans are in season, it is a favourite family
meal, served with yogurt and lots of warm, fresh crusty bread to
mop up the sauce. The taste of fresh dill is an essential part of the
dish. These olive oil dishes, which have survived from the Ottoman
Empire, include leeks cooked in olive oil, celeriac, green beans,
artichokes, and borlotti beans.

1 Put the onions, garlic and oil in a
wide heavy pan and stir over a low heat
until they soften. Toss in the beans,
coating them in the onions and oil, then
stir in the sugar and lemon juice.

2 Add the tomatoes and bring to the
boil, then lower the heat and add the
dill. Cook gently for 35–40 minutes, or
until the beans are tender and the
tomato sauce is fairly thick.

3 Season with salt and pepper to taste
before serving.

per portion Energy 141kcal/588kJ; Protein 4.5g; Carbohydrate 16.5g, of which sugars 14g; Fat 6.8g, of which saturates 1.1g; Cholesterol 0mg; Calcium 75mg; Fibre 5.7g; Sodium 20mg.

45ml/3 tbsp olive oil

15ml/1 tbsp butter

450g/1lb button (white) mushrooms, wiped clean

3–4 garlic cloves, finely chopped

10ml/2 tsp allspice berries, crushed

10ml/2 tsp coriander seeds

5ml/1 tsp dried mint

1 bunch each of fresh sage and flat leaf parsley, chopped

salt and ground black pepper

lemon wedges, to serve

SERVES 4

preparing mushrooms *Button mushrooms are ideal for this recipe as they don't release much liquid into the pan and caramelize beautifully. Don't wash the mushrooms before cooking, just wipe with a clean dish towel and keep them whole.*

caramelized mushrooms with allspice and herbs

Button mushrooms caramelize beautifully in their own juice, but still keep their moistness and nutty flavour. They are usually served as a side dish for grilled lamb chops or liver, or as a hot or cold *meze* dish with chunks of bread to mop up the tasty cooking juices, but they are also good served on toasted crusty bread as a light lunch with a salad. Use whatever herbs and spices you have available, just as they would in the different regions of Turkey.

1 Heat the oil and butter in wide, heavy pan, then stir in the mushrooms with the garlic, allspice and coriander. Cover and cook for about 10 minutes, shaking the pan from time to time, until the mushrooms start to caramelize.

2 Remove the lid and toss in the mint with some of the sage and parsley. Cook for a further 5 minutes, until most of the liquid has evaporated, then season with salt and pepper.

3 Tip the mushrooms into a serving dish and sprinkle the rest of the sage and parsley over the top. Serve hot or at room temperature, with lemon wedges for squeezing.

per portion Energy 125kcal/517kJ; Protein 2.8g; Carbohydrate 1.2g, of which sugars 0.8g; Fat 12.2g, of which saturates 3.3g; Cholesterol 8mg; Calcium 58mg; Fibre 2.5g; Sodium 37mg.

artichokes with
beans and almonds

In the early summer, markets and street-sellers display crates of globe artichokes, which the Turks love to poach in olive oil. Often the seller will have them prepared ready for poaching, or will do it while you wait. The tender bottoms are traditionally filled with fresh broad beans and flavoured with dill, but sometimes diced carrots, potatoes, whole baby shallots and fresh peas are used as a filling, or the poached artichokes are simply served by themselves with a little dill. Ready-prepared artichoke bottoms are available frozen in some supermarkets and Middle Eastern stores, otherwise follow the preparation below. Serve as an appetizer or as a side dish.

175g/6oz/2 cups shelled broad (fava) beans

4 large globe artichokes, trimmed to their bottoms (see below)

120ml/4fl oz/½ cup olive oil

juice of 1 lemon

10ml/2 tsp granulated sugar

75g/3oz/¾ cup blanched almonds

1 small bunch of fresh dill, chopped

2 tomatoes, skinned, seeded and diced

salt

SERVES 4

1 Put the beans in pan of water and bring to the boil. Lower the heat and simmer for 10–15 minutes or until tender. Drain and refresh under cold running water, then peel off the skins.

2 Place the artichokes in a heavy pan. Mix together the oil, lemon juice and 50ml/2fl oz/¼ cup water and pour over the artichokes. Cover and poach gently for about 20 minutes, then add the sugar, beans and almonds. Cover again and continue to poach gently for a further 10 minutes, or until the artichokes are tender. Toss in half the dill, season with salt, and turn off the heat. Leave the artichokes to cool in the pan.

3 Lift the artichokes out of the pan and place them hollow-side up in a serving dish. Mix the tomatoes with the beans and almonds, spoon into the middle of the artichokes and around them, and garnish with the remaining dill. Serve at room temperature.

preparing globe artichokes *Until ready to use, fresh artichokes should be treated like flowers and put in a jug (pitcher) of water. To prepare them for this dish, cut off the stalks and pull off all the leaves. Dig out the hairy choke from the middle with a spoon, then cut away any hard bits with a small sharp knife and trim into a neat cup shape. Rub the cups – called bottoms – with a mixture of lemon juice and salt to prevent them from discolouring.*

blanching almonds *Buy fresh-looking almonds in their skins. Put them in a bowl and cover with boiling water. Leave to soak for a few hours until the skins loosen, then rub the skins off with your fingers. If you leave them for as long as 24 hours, the nuts soften, too.*

per portion Energy 351kcal/1455kJ; Protein 8.2g; Carbohydrate 13.4g, of which sugars 8.3g; Fat 29.8g, of which saturates 3.6g; Cholesterol 0mg; Calcium 110mg; Fibre 5.5g; Sodium 29mg.

carrot and apricot rolls with mint yogurt

These sweet, herby carrot rolls are a great treat in Istanbul and Izmir, but rarely found elsewhere. Served with a dollop of yogurt flavoured with mint and garlic, they make a delicious light lunch or supper with a green salad and warm crusty bread. Alternatively, you can mould the mixture into miniature balls and serve them on sticks as a nibble to go with drinks, using the yogurt as a dip.

8–10 carrots, cut into thick slices

2–3 slices of day-old bread, ground into crumbs

4 spring onions (scallions), finely sliced

150g/5oz/generous ½ cup dried apricots, finely chopped or sliced

45ml/3 tbsp pine nuts

1 egg

5ml/1 tsp Turkish red pepper, or 1 fresh red chilli, seeded and finely chopped

1 bunch of fresh dill, chopped

1 bunch of fresh basil, finely shredded

salt and ground black pepper

plain (all-purpose) flour, for coating

sunflower oil, for shallow frying

lemon wedges, to serve

FOR THE MINT YOGURT

about 225g/8oz/1 cup thick and creamy natural (plain) yogurt

juice of ½ lemon

1–2 garlic cloves, crushed

1 bunch of fresh mint, finely chopped

SERVES 4

1 Steam the carrot slices for about 25 minutes, or until they are very soft. Do not boil them as they will become too watery, and then they will lose some of their flavour and natural sweetness.

2 While the carrots are steaming, make the mint yogurt. Beat the yogurt in a bowl with the lemon juice and garlic, season with salt and pepper and stir in the mint. Set aside, or chill in the refrigerator.

3 Mash the carrots to a paste while they are warm. Add the breadcrumbs, spring onions, apricots and pine nuts and mix well with a fork. Beat in the egg and stir in the red pepper or chilli and herbs. Season with salt and pepper.

4 Tip a small heap of flour on to a flat surface. Take a plum-sized portion of the carrot mixture in your fingers and mould it into an oblong roll. If the mixture is very sticky, make it easier to deal with by adding more breadcrumbs or wetting your hands. Coat the carrot roll in the flour and put it on a plate. Repeat with rest of the mixture, to get 12–16 rolls altogether.

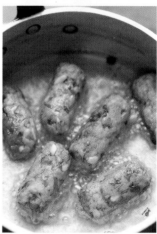

5 Heat enough sunflower oil for shallow frying in a heavy frying pan. Place the carrot rolls in the hot oil and fry over a medium heat for 8–10 minutes, turning them from time to time, until they are golden brown on all sides. Remove with a slotted spoon and drain on kitchen paper. Serve the rolls hot, with lemon wedges and the mint yogurt.

per portion Energy 401kcal/1673kJ; Protein 8.7g; Carbohydrate 46g, of which sugars 29.1g; Fat 21.5g, of which saturates 2.5g; Cholesterol 48mg; Calcium 144mg; Fibre 8.5g; Sodium 145mg.

potatoes baked with tomatoes, olives, feta and oregano

This tasty potato dish comes from western Anatolia. Traditionally baked in an earthenware dish, it makes a fabulous accompaniment to meat, poultry or fish. Or serve it on its own as a main course with a squeeze of lemon or a dollop of yogurt, and a green salad.

675g/1½lb organic new potatoes

15ml/1 tbsp butter

45ml/3 tbsp olive oil

2 red onions, cut in half lengthways, in half again crossways, and sliced along the grain

3–4 garlic cloves, chopped

5–10ml/1–2 tsp cumin seeds, crushed

5–10ml/1–2 tsp Turkish red pepper, or 1 fresh red chilli, seeded and chopped

10ml/2 tsp dried oregano

10ml/2 tsp sugar

15ml/1 tbsp white wine vinegar

400g/14oz can chopped tomatoes, drained of juice

12–16 black olives

115g/4oz feta cheese, crumbled

salt and ground black pepper

extra olive oil, for drizzling

1 lemon, cut into wedges

SERVES 4–6

1 Preheat the oven to 200°C/400°F/Gas 6. Put the potatoes into a pan of cold water, bring to the boil and cook for 15–20 minutes, or until tender but not soft. Drain and refresh under cold running water, then peel off the skins and cut the potatoes into thick slices or bitesize wedges.

2 Heat the butter and 30ml/2 tbsp of the oil in a heavy pan, stir in the onions and garlic and cook until soft. Add the cumin seeds, red pepper or chilli and most of the oregano – reserve a little for the top – then stir in the sugar and vinegar, followed by the tomatoes. Season with salt and pepper.

3 Put the potatoes and olives into a baking dish – preferably an earthenware one – and spoon the tangy tomato mixture over them. Crumble the feta on top and sprinkle with the reserved oregano. Drizzle with the remaining oil, then bake for 25–30 minutes.

4 Serve hot, with lemon wedges to squeeze over.

per portion Energy 243kcal/1016kJ; Protein 6.3g; Carbohydrate 27.5g, of which sugars 9.3g; Fat 12.8g, of which saturates 5g; Cholesterol 19mg; Calcium 102mg; Fibre 2.9g; Sodium 447mg.

kabak mucver

Ideal for lunch, supper, a savoury snack or appetizer, these tasty patties are incredibly versatile. You can even make miniature ones and serve them as a nibble with drinks. If you like a little fire on your tongue, add more Turkish red pepper or chillies.

1 Wash the courgettes and trim off the ends. Hold them at an angle and grate them, then put them in a colander or sieve (strainer) and sprinkle with a little salt. Leave them to weep for 5 minutes.

2 Squeeze the grated courgettes in your hand to extract the juices. Heat the olive oil in a heavy frying pan, stir in the courgettes, onion and garlic and fry until they begin to take on colour. Remove from the heat and leave to cool.

3 Tip the flour into a bowl and gradually beat in the eggs to form a smooth batter. Beat in the cooled courgette mixture. Add the feta, herbs and red pepper or chilli, and season with a little pepper. Add salt if you like, but usually the feta is quite salty. Mix well.

4 Heat enough sunflower oil for shallow frying in a heavy, non-stick pan. Drop four spoonfuls of the mixture into the hot oil, leaving space between each one, then fry over a medium heat for 6–8 minutes, or until firm to the touch and golden brown on both sides. Remove from the pan with a slotted spoon and drain on kitchen paper while you fry the remainder.

5 Serve while still warm, garnished with mint leaves.

3 firm courgettes (zucchini)

30–45ml/2–3 tbsp olive oil

1 large onion, cut in half lengthways, in half again crossways, and sliced along the grain

4 garlic cloves, chopped

45ml/3 tbsp plain (all-purpose) flour

3 eggs, beaten

225g/8oz feta cheese, crumbled

1 bunch each of fresh flat leaf parsley, mint and dill, chopped

5ml/1 tsp Turkish red pepper, or 1 fresh red chilli, seeded and chopped

sunflower oil, for shallow frying

salt and ground black pepper

mint leaves, to garnish

SERVES 4–6

per portion Energy 327kcal/1354kJ; Protein 12.3g; Carbohydrate 12.4g, of which sugars 5.4g; Fat 25.7g, of which saturates 7.9g; Cholesterol 121mg; Calcium 214mg; Fibre 2.3g; Sodium 581mg.

roasted courgettes and peaches with pine nuts

A favourite dish in Turkey is a mixture of deep-fried or grilled vegetables served with a garlic-flavoured sauce made with yogurt, nuts or sesame paste. Courgettes, aubergines and carrots are the most common vegetables used, and they are often deep-fried in batter. This recipe combines fruit and vegetables to make a colourful medley that is baked rather than deep-fried or grilled, and given the option to serve it with a yogurt or *tarator* sauce, or a tahini dressing. Serve with warm, crusty bread, or as an accompaniment to grilled, broiled or barbecued meats and poultry.

2 courgettes (zucchini)

2 yellow or red (bell) peppers, seeded and cut into wedges

100ml/3½ fl oz/scant ½ cup olive oil

4–6 plum tomatoes

2 firm peaches, peeled, halved and stoned (pitted), then cut into wedges

30ml/2 tbsp pine nuts

salt and ground black pepper

FOR THE YOGURT SAUCE

500g/1¼ lb/2¼ cups thick and creamy natural (plain) yogurt

2–3 garlic cloves, crushed

juice of ½ lemon

SERVES 4

1 Preheat the oven to 200°C/400°F/Gas 6. Using a vegetable peeler or a small, sharp knife, peel the courgettes lengthways in stripes like a zebra, then halve and slice them lengthways, or cut into wedges.

2 Place the courgettes and peppers in a baking dish, preferably an earthenware one. Drizzle the oil over them and sprinkle with salt, then bake in the oven for 20 minutes.

3 Take the dish out of the oven and turn the vegetables in the oil, then mix in the tomatoes and peaches. Bake for another 20–25 minutes, until everything is nicely browned.

4 Meanwhile, make the yogurt sauce. In a bowl, beat the yogurt with the garlic and lemon juice. Season with salt and pepper and set aside, or chill in the refrigerator.

5 Dry-roast the pine nuts in a small, heavy pan until they turn golden brown and give off a nutty aroma. Remove from the heat.

6 When the roasted vegetables are ready, remove the dish from the oven and sprinkle the pine nuts over the top. Serve with the yogurt sauce.

tahini dressing *Thin down about 30ml/2 tbsp sesame paste with a little water and lemon juice; beat in some crushed garlic and, if you like, a little roasted Turkish red pepper. Season with salt and pepper.*

per portion Energy 362kcal/1507kJ; Protein 11.7g; Carbohydrate 26.7g, of which sugars 26.3g; Fat 24.1g, of which saturates 3.7g; Cholesterol 2mg; Calcium 284mg; Fibre 4.8g; Sodium 120mg.

elma dolması

Vegetables and fruit stuffed with an aromatic pilaff are a great favourite in Turkey. Anything with a cavity can be stuffed – and if there is no cavity, you should make one. Aubergines, courgettes, tomatoes, apples and plums are all stuffed with aromatic rice, or with a mixture of rice and minced meat. This recipe is for apples, but you can easily use it to make an impressive medley of stuffed fruit and vegetables for a buffet.

4 cooking apples, or any firm, sour apple of your choice

30ml/2 tbsp olive oil

juice of ½ lemon

10ml/2 tsp sugar

salt and ground black pepper

FOR THE FILLING

30ml/2 tbsp olive oil

a little butter

1 onion, finely chopped

2 garlic cloves

30ml/2 tbsp pine nuts

30ml/2 tbsp currants, soaked in warm water for 5–10 minutes and drained

5–10ml/1–2 tsp ground cinnamon

5–10ml/1–2 tsp ground allspice

5ml/1 tsp sugar

175g/6oz/scant 1 cup short grain rice, thoroughly rinsed and drained

1 bunch each of fresh flat leaf parsley and dill, finely chopped

TO SERVE

1 tomato

1 lemon

a few fresh mint or basil leaves

SERVES 4

1 Make the filling. Heat the oil and butter in a heavy pan, stir in the onion and garlic and cook until they soften. Add the pine nuts and currants and cook until the nuts turn golden.

2 Stir in the spices, sugar and rice, and mix well. Pour in enough water to cover the rice – roughly 1–2cm/½–¾in above the grains – and bring to the boil. Season with salt and pepper and stir, then lower the heat and simmer for about 10–12 minutes, until almost all the water has been absorbed.

3 Toss in the herbs and turn off the heat. Cover the pan with a dry dish towel and the lid, and leave the rice to steam for 5 minutes.

4 Preheat the oven to 200°C/400°F/ Gas 6. Using a sharp knife, cut the stalk ends off the apples and keep to use as lids. Carefully core each apple, removing some of the flesh to create a wide enough cavity to stuff.

5 Take spoonfuls of the rice and pack it into the apples. Replace the lids and stand the apples, upright and tightly packed, in a small baking dish.

6 In a jug (pitcher), mix together 100ml/3½fl oz/scant ½ cup water with the oil, lemon juice and sugar. Pour this mixture over and around the apples, then bake for 30–40 minutes, until the apples are tender and the cooking juices are slightly caramelized.

7 Serve with a tomato and lemon garnish and a sprinkling of mint or basil leaves.

per portion Energy 382kcal/1595kJ; Protein 5g; Carbohydrate 54.1g, of which sugars 18.8g; Fat 16.5g, of which saturates 1.9g; Cholesterol 0mg; Calcium 26mg; Fibre 2.1g; Sodium 4mg.

PILAFFS, BEANS AND LENTILS

black-eyed bean stew with spicy sausage

garlic-flavoured lentils with carrots
and sage

zeytinyağlı barbunya

Anatolian bulgur with nuts and dates

pumpkin stuffed with saffron
and apricot pilaff

aubergine pilaff with cinnamon and mint

hamsili pilav

sultan's chickpea pilaff

sour cherry pilaff

pilaffs, beans and lentils

The pillars of elaborate feasts, as well as the staple diet of the poor, grain, bean and lentil dishes play a key role – served as palate cleansers, side dishes, or as meals on their own.

The Turks eat rice, bulgur, beans and lentils every day, but it has not always been that way: bulgur and beans were established in the early history of Anatolia, but rice is relatively new. The migrating Turkic tribes would have taken rice to Persia from China and India, but it didn't really make an impact on Anatolia and Constantinople until the Ottoman era, when the wealthy imported large quantities of rice from Egypt. Still more expensive than bulgur and couscous, rice continues to play second fiddle to wheat grains in parts of Anatolia, but it is the principal grain in Ankara, Istanbul and Izmir, and in much of western Turkey.

The Turkish concept of *pilav* is thought to have originated from the Persian tradition of *pulaw* dishes, but it has developed into a class of its own and spread across all social divides throughout the country – so much so, in fact, that no wedding feast neglects to include a pilaff of some description, as well as *zerde*, a jelly-like rice pudding flavoured and coloured with saffron.

Pilaff made with rice is a well-known Turkish speciality, but the lesser-known pilaff made with bulgur is just as common, particularly in rural Anatolia. Vegetables and meat – peas, carrots, chicken and mutton – are often added to the rice or bulgur to make substantial dishes that are eaten on their own, while lamb's liver is combined with rice in the famous *iç pilav* (liver pilaff) from Istanbul.

A pilaff that is going to be served cold, such as the popular aromatic aubergine (eggplant) rice made in Istanbul, is usually made with olive oil. Some pilaff dishes call for the inclusion of small pasta shapes the size of teardrops, and these make a filling, homely meal that children adore, while dried beans, peas and lentils – chickpeas and red lentils in particular– can also be added to rice, as in the Ottoman dish *Sultan Reşat pilavı*, made with rice and chickpeas. For colour and flavour, many rice and bulgur dishes include tiny black currants, roasted nuts and dried fruits, such as apricots, dates or figs. In some homes, plain pilaffs may be served last, after the sweet dish, to cleanse the palate of sugary tastes – following the principles of the Topkapı Palace kitchens.

The cooking of rice is regarded as an art. The grains must be soft, but still have a bite to them, as well as having absorbed any flavours in the

Above, from left to right
Black-eyed bean (pea) stew,
pumpkin, zeytinyağlı barbunya.

dish. As a rule, the grains and other ingredients are cooked in a little butter, ghee or oil before the water is added, then, once the water has been absorbed, a cloth or dish towel is placed on top of the pan followed by a tight-fitting lid. The rice is then left to steam off the heat until the grains are cooked but still firm. Depending on the grain, the ratio of rice to water is generally equal, or the volume of the water may be one and a half times that of the rice. Long grain rice from Iran, Syria or Turkey itself is preferred for pilaffs, while the shorter grains are reserved for the aromatic savoury fillings that are stuffed into vegetables and fruits, and for sweet puddings like the popular *sütlaç*.

Whether made with rice or bulgur, or a combination of grain, beans and lentils, Turkish pilaffs are usually served hot, the exception being the aubergine (eggplant) and olive oil pilaff made in Istanbul. Sometimes extra butter or ghee is melted and poured over the hot pilaff at the end, just before serving. One of the most popular snacks in eastern Anatolia is a bowl of cooked bulgur with a hole in the middle into which yogurt is spooned and then melted ghee poured over the top. Everyone takes a spoon and dives in.

There are traditional names for specific methods of cooking rice and bulgur to which many cooks adhere. *Salma* is the simplest method: the grains are simmered in water or stock until almost all the liquid is absorbed, then the pan is covered and the grains are left to steam. *Kavurma* involves frying additional ingredients and flavourings in butter, oil or sheep's tail fat before stirring in the uncooked grains, followed by the liquid, and then simmering until the liquid is absorbed. For *buryani*, grains that have been cooked using the *salma* method are tossed over a high heat with chunks of meat, shellfish, or vegetables, and are often flavoured with spices.

The Turkish word *bakliyat*, meaning beans, peas and lentils, derives from the Arabic word *bakli*, which means vegetable. Regarded as a vegetable, *bakliyat* dishes of all kinds are immensely popular in Turkish cooking, served as snacks and *meze*, meals on their own with bread, or in place of rice to accompany a main dish. In poor rural areas, they are often cooked as the staple ingredient in place of meat. The main ones used are dried haricot (navy), soya and borlotti beans, broad (fava) beans, black-eyed beans (peas), chickpeas, red and green lentils and split peas.

Beans are held in such high regard in Turkey that they are considered to be "food from heaven", borne out by the old Turkish saying, "he thinks he is as blessed as a bean."

Above, from left to right
Hamsili pilav, *Sultan's chickpea pilaff, rice.*

black-eyed bean stew
with spicy sausage

Bean stews made with spicy cured sausage, or cured, dried beef fillet, are popular family and workmen's café dishes. In the Aegean region, meaty black-eyed beans are used, but any dried beans or chickpeas may be substituted. Traditionally, the stew is cooked in a heavy earthenware pot that is brought to the table for everyone to help themselves – dipping chunks of fresh, crusty bread into the tasty sauce. A typical accompaniment would be a salad with hot green peppers and parsley, or pickled vegetables.

175g/6oz/scant 1 cup dried black-eyed beans (peas), soaked in cold water overnight

30ml/2 tbsp ghee or 15ml/1 tbsp each olive oil and butter

1 large onion, cut in half lengthways and sliced along the grain

2–3 garlic cloves, roughly chopped and bruised with the flat side of a knife

5ml/1 tsp cumin seeds

5–10ml/1–2 tsp coriander seeds

5ml/1 tsp fennel seeds

5–10ml/1–2 tsp sugar or clear honey

1 spicy cured sausage, about 25cm/10in long (see below), sliced

150ml/¼ pint/⅔ cup white wine

400g/14oz can tomatoes

1 bunch of fresh flat leaf parsley, roughly chopped

salt and ground black pepper

SERVES 4–6

1 Drain the beans, tip them into a pan and fill the pan with plenty of cold water. Bring to the boil and boil for 1 minute, then lower the heat and partially cover the pan. Simmer the beans for about 25 minutes, or until they are al dente. Drain, rinse well under cold running water and remove any loose skins.

2 Preheat the oven to 180°C/350°F/ Gas 4. Melt the ghee in a heavy pan or flameproof earthenware pot. Stir in the onion, garlic and spices and fry until the onion begins to colour.

3 Stir in the sugar or honey, toss in the spicy sausage and cook until it begins to brown.

4 Add the beans, followed by the wine. Bubble up the wine, then lower the heat and add the tomatoes. Stir in half the parsley and season with salt and pepper.

5 Cover and bake for about 40 minutes. Before serving, taste for seasoning and sprinkle with the remaining parsley.

pastırma This dish can also be made with pastırma – a cured fillet of beef encased in çemen, which is a dark red paste made from groun fenugreek, cumin, red pepper and garlic. Hanging like paddles, pastırma is a feature of the charcuterie section of every market.

spicy cured sausage For this recipe use any Turkish, Greek or Italian spicy sausage. The Turkish sucuk is horseshoe-shaped and spiked with cumin, while the long pastırma fillets are coated in fenugreek. Both are sold in Middle Eastern shops.

per portion Energy 382kcal/1594kJ; Protein 18g; Carbohydrate 20g, of which sugars 6.7g; Fat 24.4g, of which saturates 10g; Cholesterol 52mg; Calcium 55mg; Fibre 6g; Sodium 944mg.

garlic-flavoured lentils with carrots and sage

Adapted from one of the Ottoman *zeytinyağlı* dishes, which is flavoured with mint and dill, this simple recipe uses sage instead. In Anatolia, pungent sage leaves are dried in the sun, which captures their strong herby aroma, and stalks of dried sage are tied in bunches and sold in the markets to make a restorative tea. The same sage is ideal for cooking, as its warming flavour spreads through the dish. Serve these lentils with grilled, broiled or barbecued meats, or on their own with a dollop of yogurt seasoned with crushed garlic, salt and pepper, and lemon wedges.

175g/6oz/¾ cup green lentils, rinsed and picked over

45–60ml/3–4 tbsp fruity olive oil

1 onion, cut in half lengthways, in half again crossways, and sliced along the grain

3–4 plump garlic cloves, roughly chopped and bruised with the flat side of a knife

5ml/1 tsp coriander seeds

a handful of dried sage leaves

5–10ml/1–2 tsp sugar

4 carrots, sliced

15–30ml/1–2 tbsp tomato purée (paste)

salt and ground black pepper

1 bunch of fresh sage or flat leaf parsley, to garnish

SERVES 4–6

1 Bring a pan of water to the boil and tip in the lentils. Lower the heat, partially cover the pan and simmer for 10 minutes. Drain and rinse well under cold running water.

2 Heat the oil in a heavy pan, stir in the onion, garlic, coriander, sage and sugar, and cook until the onion begins to colour. Toss in the carrots and cook for 2–3 minutes.

3 Add the lentils and pour in 250ml/8fl oz/1 cup water, making sure the lentils and carrots are covered. Stir in the tomato purée and cover the pan, then cook the lentils and carrots gently for about 20 minutes, until most of the liquid has been absorbed. The lentils and carrots should both be tender, but still have some bite. Season with salt and pepper to taste.

4 Garnish with the fresh sage or flat leaf parsley, and serve hot or at room temperature.

zeytinyağlı **dishes** *Cooked in olive oil and almost always served cold, zeytinyağlı dishes include leeks and carrots, celeriac, runner or green beans, and artichokes.*

per portion Energy 166kcal/696kJ; Protein 7.6g; Carbohydrate 21.1g, of which sugars 6.7g; Fat 6.2g, of which saturates 0.9g; Cholesterol 0mg; Calcium 38mg; Fibre 4g; Sodium 22mg.

175g/6oz/scant 1 cup dried borlotti beans, soaked in cold water overnight

45–60ml/3–4 tbsp olive oil

2 red onions, cut in half lengthways, in half again crossways, and sliced along the grain

4 garlic cloves, chopped

400g/14oz can tomatoes

10ml/2 tsp sugar

1 bunch each of fresh flat leaf parsley and dill, coarsely chopped

4 ripe plum tomatoes

salt and ground black pepper

1 lemon, cut into quarters

SERVES 4

zeytinyağlı barbunya

This is a great favourite – in the markets they sell meaty, pinkish borlotti beans in their dappled pods just for preparing this dish. In poor homes, where meat may be served infrequently, dishes made from borlotti beans and aubergines make a regular appearance as a substitute. Cooked in lots of olive oil, this is another *zeytinyağlı* dish, which you will encounter all over the western region of Turkey.

1   Drain the beans, tip them into a pan and fill the pan with plenty of cold water. Bring to the boil and boil for 1 minute, then lower the heat and partially cover the pan. Simmer the beans for about 30 minutes, or until they are tender but not soft or mushy. Drain, rinse well under cold running water and remove any loose skins.

2   Heat the oil in a heavy pan and stir in the onions and garlic. When they begin to soften, add the tomatoes, sugar and half the herbs. Toss in the beans, pour in 300ml/½ pint/1¼ cups water and bring to the boil. Lower the heat and partially cover the pan, then simmer for about 20 minutes, until most of the liquid has gone.

3   Meanwhile, bring a small pan of water to the boil, drop in the tomatoes for a few seconds, then plunge them into a bowl of cold water. Peel off the skins and coarsely chop the tomatoes.

4   Add the tomatoes to the beans with the rest of the herbs – reserving a little for the garnish. Season and cook for a further 5–10 minutes. Serve hot or at room temperature, with lemon wedges for squeezing.

per portion Energy 266kcal/1119kJ; Protein 12.4g; Carbohydrate 34.4g, of which sugars 14.4g; Fat 9.8g, of which saturates 1.5g; Cholesterol 0mg; Calcium 103mg; Fibre 10.6g; Sodium 33mg.

Anatolian bulgur
with nuts and dates

There are several hearty Anatolian dishes made with rice or bulgur that include vegetables, dried fruit and nuts. This one is often attributed to the Bedouin, nomadic herdsmen in the deserts of Arabia and North Africa who depended heavily on dates.

1 Put the bulgur into a bowl, pour over enough boiling water to cover it by 2.5cm/1in, and give it a quick stir. Cover the bowl and leave the bulgur to steam for about 25 minutes, until it has soaked up the water and doubled in volume.

2 Meanwhile, melt the ghee in a wide, heavy pan, add the carrots and fry for about 10 minutes, until tender and golden. Toss in the nuts and cook for a further minute, or until they give off a nutty aroma and begin to colour.

3 Add the dates and, if they look dry, splash in 15–30ml/1–2 tbsp water. Tip the bulgur into the pan and toss until everything is mixed well together. Turn off the heat, cover the pan with a dish towel and lid, and leave to steam for 5–10 minutes.

4 To serve, stir the coriander through the bulgur, and pour over the melted ghee or butter if you like. Hand round yogurt in a small bowl.

350g/12oz/2 cups coarse-grain bulgur wheat, rinsed and drained

30ml/2 tbsp ghee

2 medium carrots, cut into matchsticks

75g/3oz/¾ cup blanched almonds

30–45ml/2–3 tbsp pine nuts

30–45ml/2–3 tbsp shelled pistachio nuts, chopped

175g/6oz/1 cup soft dried dates, roughly chopped

salt

TO SERVE

a handful of fresh coriander (cilantro), chopped

about 25g/1oz/2 tbsp ghee or butter, melted (optional)

thick and creamy natural (plain) yogurt

SERVES 4–6

Eastern Anatolian traditions
In Bedouin camps in eastern Turkey this dish is piled in a mound with yogurt spooned into a hollow and eaten communally.

per portion Energy 412kcal/1719kJ; Protein 9g; Carbohydrate 54g, of which sugars 23.4g; Fat 19.1g, of which saturates 3.9g; Cholesterol 11mg; Calcium 71mg; Fibre 3.4g; Sodium 74mg.

pumpkin stuffed with
saffron and apricot pilaff

In Cappadocia, where there is an extraordinary landscape of troglodyte cave dwellings, fairy chimneys and churches carved out of the rock, extensive use is made of pumpkins and apricots in cooking. Pumpkins make ideal cooking vessels, filled with aromatic pilaffs as in this recipe, or with meat and rice, vegetables or soup. This sumptuous fruit and nut pilaff would normally be reserved for special occasions, such as a wedding feast.

1 Preheat the oven to 200°C/400°F/ Gas 6. Wash the pumpkin and cut off the stalk end to use as a lid. Scoop all the seeds out of the middle with a metal spoon, and pull out the stringy bits. Replace the lid, put the pumpkin on a baking tray and bake for 1 hour.

2 Meanwhile, tip the rice into a pan and pour in just enough water to cover. Add a pinch of salt and bring to the boil, then lower the heat and partially cover the pan. Simmer for 10–12 minutes, until all the water has been absorbed and the grains of rice are cooked but still have a bite.

3 Heat the oil and butter in a wide, heavy pan. Stir in the saffron, coriander seeds, orange zest, pistachios, cranberries and apricots, then toss in the cooked rice, making sure everything is well mixed, and season with salt and pepper. Turn off the heat, cover the pan with a dish towel and press the lid tightly on top. Leave the pilaff to steam for 10 minutes, then toss in the herbs.

4 Take the pumpkin out of the oven. Lift off the lid and spoon the pilaff into the cavity. Put the lid back on and pop it back in the oven for about 20 minutes.

5 To serve, remove the lid and slice a round off the top of the pumpkin. Place the ring on a plate and spoon some pilaff in the middle. Continue slicing and filling on individual plates until all the pumpkin and pilaff are used up. Serve with lemon wedges and a bowl of yogurt.

1 medium-sized pumpkin, weighing about 1.2kg/2½lb

225g/8oz/generous 1 cup long grain rice, well rinsed

30–45ml/2–3 tbsp olive oil

15ml/1 tbsp butter

a fingerful of saffron threads

5ml/1 tsp coriander seeds

2–3 strips of orange peel, pith removed and finely sliced

45–60ml/3–4 tbsp shelled pistachio nuts

30–45ml/2–3 tbsp dried cranberries, soaked in boiling water for 5 minutes and drained

175g/6oz/¾ cup dried apricots, sliced or chopped

1 bunch of fresh basil, leaves loosely torn

1 bunch each of fresh coriander, mint and flat leaf parsley, coarsely chopped

salt and ground black pepper

lemon wedges and thick and creamy natural (plain) yogurt, to serve

SERVES 4–6

per portion Energy 345kcal/1443kJ; Protein 9.9g; Carbohydrate 50.1g, of which sugars 18.6g; Fat 12g, of which saturates 2.6g; Cholesterol 5mg; Calcium 299mg; Fibre 9.6g; Sodium 93mg.

aubergine pilaff with cinnamon and mint

This wonderful rice dish varies from region to region. In Istanbul, where it is known as *Sultan Reşat pilavı*, it is made with olive oil and served cold. Variations may use bulgur, or tiny pasta "tears" cooked with the rice, but all recipes include meaty chunks of aubergine. Eat it on its own accompanied by a green salad, or serve it with grilled, broiled or barbecued meat.

1 Using a vegetable peeler or a small, sharp knife, peel the aubergines lengthways in stripes like a zebra. Quarter them lengthways, then slice each quarter into bitesize chunks and place in a bowl of salted water. Cover with a plate to keep them submerged, and leave to soak for at least 30 minutes.

2 Meanwhile, heat the olive oil in a heavy pan, stir in the pine nuts and cook until they turn golden. Add the onion and soften it, then stir in the coriander seeds and currants. Add the sugar, cinnamon, mint and dill and stir in the tomatoes.

3 Toss in the rice, coating it well in the tomato and spices, then pour in 900ml/ 1½ pints/3¾ cups water, season with salt and pepper and bring to the boil. Lower the heat and partially cover the pan, then simmer for 10–12 minutes, until almost all of the water has been absorbed. Turn off the heat, cover the pan with a dish towel and press the lid tightly on top. Leave the rice to steam for about 15 minutes.

4 Heat enough sunflower oil for deep-frying in a wok or other deep-sided pan. Drain the aubergines and squeeze them dry, then toss them in batches in the oil, for a few minutes at a time. When they are golden brown, lift them out with a slotted spoon and drain on kitchen paper.

5 Tip the rice into a serving bowl and toss the aubergine chunks through it with the lemon juice. Garnish with fresh mint sprigs and serve warm or cold, with lemon wedges for squeezing.

2 large aubergines (eggplants)

30–45ml/2–3 tbsp olive oil

30–45ml/2–3 tbsp pine nuts

1 large onion, finely chopped

5ml/1 tsp coriander seeds

30ml/2 tbsp currants, soaked in warm water for 5–10 minutes and drained

10–15ml/2–3 tsp sugar

15–30ml/1–2 tbsp ground cinnamon

15–30ml/1–2 tbsp dried mint

1 small bunch of fresh dill, finely chopped

3 tomatoes, skinned, seeded and finely chopped

350g/12oz/generous 1¾ cups long or short grain rice, well rinsed and drained

sunflower oil, for deep-frying

juice of ½ lemon

salt and ground black pepper

fresh mint sprigs and lemon wedges, to serve

SERVES 4–6

per portion Energy 369kcal/1539kJ; Protein 6.1g; Carbohydrate 52.2g, of which sugars 11g; Fat 15.2g, of which saturates 1.8g; Cholesterol 0mg; Calcium 38mg; Fibre 2.7g; Sodium 8mg.

hamsili pilav

Packed full of anchovies, this famous rice dish is from the Black Sea coast, where anchovies are used in many dishes and written about in songs and poetry. There are several ways of making it: whole anchovies can be fried and tossed through the rice, the anchovies and rice can be layered and baked, or the anchovies can be boned, as here, and used to line a dish in which the rice is baked.

600g/1lb 6oz fresh anchovies, gutted, with heads and backbones removed

30ml/2 tbsp olive oil

15ml/1 tbsp butter

1 onion, finely chopped

30ml/2 tbsp pine nuts

15ml/1 tbsp dried mint

5ml/1 tsp ground allspice

450g/1lb/2¼ cups long grain rice, thoroughly rinsed and drained

1 small bunch of fresh dill, finely chopped

salt and ground black pepper

fresh dill fronds and lemon wedges, to serve

SERVES 4–6

1 Rinse the anchovies and pat dry. Open them out like butterflies and sprinkle with salt. Lightly grease a dome-shaped ovenproof dish or bowl and line it with anchovies, skin side down. Reserve some anchovies for the top.

2 Heat the oil and butter in a heavy pan, stir in the onion and cook until soft. Add the pine nuts and cook until golden, then stir in the mint, allspice and rice. Season, and pour in enough water to cover the rice by 2cm/¾in. Bring to the boil, lower the heat, partially cover and simmer for 10–12 minutes, until the water has been absorbed.

3 While the rice is cooking, preheat the oven to 180°C/350°F/Gas 4.

4 Turn off the heat under the pan and sprinkle the dill over the rice. Cover the pan with a dish towel, put the lid tightly on top and leave the rice to steam for 10 minutes.

5 Fluff up the rice with a fork to mix in the dill, then tip it into the anchovy mould. Lay the remaining anchovies, skin side up this time, over the rice. Splash a little water over the top and place the dish in the oven for about 25 minutes.

6 To serve, invert a serving plate over the dish and turn out the anchovy mould encasing the rice. Garnish with dill fronds and lemon wedges and serve immediately, on its own or as an accompaniment to a fish dish.

per portion Energy 481kcal/2004kJ; Protein 19.5g; Carbohydrate 64g, of which sugars 3g; Fat 16g, of which saturates 3.1g; Cholesterol 37mg; Calcium 178mg; Fibre 0.8g; Sodium 1982mg.

sultan's chickpea pilaff

There is a story that Mahmut Pasha, the Grand Vizier of Mehmet the Conqueror, used to invite his ministers to lunch every Friday, when he would serve a special mound of rice and chickpea pilaff at the end of the meal. As each minister dipped into the rice with his spoon, solid gold balls the same size as the chickpeas would be revealed, bringing good fortune to those who managed to get one on their spoon. A classic buttery pilaff, fit for a sultan, this dish is a perfect accompaniment to almost any meat or fish dish.

50g/2oz/⅓ cup dried chickpeas, soaked in cold water overnight

30ml/2 tbsp butter

15ml/1 tbsp olive or sunflower oil

1 onion, chopped

225g/8oz/generous 1 cup long grain rice, well rinsed and drained

600ml/1 pint/2½ cups water or chicken stock

salt and ground black pepper

SERVES 4

1 Drain the chickpeas, tip them into a pan and fill the pan with plenty of cold water. Bring to the boil and boil for 1 minute, then lower the heat and partially cover the pan. Simmer the chickpeas for about 45 minutes, or until tender. Drain, rinse well under cold running water and remove any loose skins.

2 Melt the butter with the oil in a heavy pan, stir in the onion and cook until it softens. Add the rice and chickpeas and cover with the water or stock. Season with salt and pepper and bring to the boil. Lower the heat, partially cover the pan and simmer for 10–12 minutes, until almost all of the water has been absorbed.

3 Turn off the heat, cover the pan with a dish towel and put the lid tightly on top. Leave the rice to steam for 10 minutes, then fluff up with a fork before serving.

per portion Energy 328kcal/1368kJ; Protein 7.1g; Carbohydrate 52.3g, of which sugars 1.2g; Fat 9.9g, of which saturates 4.4g; Cholesterol 16mg; Calcium 36mg; Fibre 1.6g; Sodium 51mg.

sour cherry pilaff

This is a popular summer pilaff made with small, sour cherries rather than the plump, sweet ones. With its refreshing bursts of cherry, it goes with most vegetable, meat and fish dishes.

30ml/2 tbsp butter

225g/8oz fresh sour cherries, such as morello, pitted

5–10ml/1–2 tsp sugar

5ml/1 tsp caraway seeds

225g/8oz/generous 1 cup long grain rice, well rinsed and drained

salt and ground black pepper

SERVES 3–4

1 Melt the butter in a heavy pan. Set a handful of the cherries aside, and toss the rest in the butter with the sugar and caraway seeds. Cook for a few minutes, then add the rice and 600ml/1 pint/2½ cups water. Season with salt and pepper.

2 Bring to the boil, lower the heat and partially cover the pan. Simmer for 10–12 minutes, until most of the water has been absorbed. Turn off the heat, cover with a dish towel, and put the lid tightly on top. Leave for 20 minutes.

3 Fluff up the rice with a fork, tip on to a serving dish and garnish with the reserved cherries.

sour cherries *Due to their acidity, sour cherries are often consumed cooked or poached with sugar in sorbets, jam, bread pudding, cakes, and in a pretty compôte that is traditionally spooned over rice or yogurt. If fresh sour cherries are not available, dried cherries can be substituted for this recipe.*

per portion Energy 295kcal/1231kJ; Protein 4.7g; Carbohydrate 54g, of which sugars 9.1g; Fat 6.5g, of which saturates 3.9g; Cholesterol 16mg; Calcium 21mg; Fibre 0.5g; Sodium 46mg.

FISH AND SHELLFISH

chargrilled sardines in vine leaves

baked sardines with tomatoes, thyme
and purple basil

kiliç şiş

mackerel pilaki

sea bass baked in salt

cinnamon fishcakes with currants,
pine nuts and herbs

uskumru dolması

Mediterranean squid with olives
and red wine

karides güveç

mussels stuffed with aromatic pilaff
and pine nuts

fish and shellfish

In the coastal regions, shark, swordfish, tuna, sea bass, mackerel, red mullet, squid and prawns are just some of the fish and shellfish that grace the modern Turkish table.

Bounded on three sides by sea – the Aegean, the Mediterranean and the Black Sea – with the Sea of Marmara and its waterways, the Bosphorus and the Dardanelles, Turkey has over 7,000km/ 4,350 miles of coastline and no shortage of fishing waters providing daily catches of bluefish, red and grey mullet, swordfish, sea bass, bonito, tuna, turbot, plaice, mackerel, sardines, anchovies and all manner of shellfish. Regarded as a symbol of fertility, fish is much enjoyed in the coastal regions of Turkey. In Istanbul and Izmir, and in the southern tourist centres of Bodrum, Antalya and Marmaris, there are numerous fish restaurants and some superbly inventive cooks.

The Black Sea coast has its own unique fish cuisine, mainly revolving around the anchovy, *hamsi*, which is celebrated in song and poetry – and in recipes like anchovy rice and anchovy bread. Inland, in the heart of Anatolia, fish is not eaten so regularly as on the coast, for obvious reasons, although carp are fished from the rivers.

Above, from left to right
Kiliç şiş, *sardines, mussels stuffed with aromatic pilaff and pine nuts.*

The *pilaki* dishes are the most distinctive of the Turkish fish dishes. These are made by sautéing onion, garlic, carrot and celery, or celeriac, in olive oil, then adding the fish along with salt, water and sugar and cooking it until tender. All *pilaki* dishes, including those that are made with beans or mussels, are cooked this way, but a dish that seems to have disappeared from the culinary scene is oyster *pilaki*, which was an old Ottoman favourite.

A decadent dish from the Palace kitchens is *uskumru dolması* (stuffed mackerel), for which the fish is pummelled and massaged to loosen the flesh from the skin. After spewing out of an opening made at the head end of the fish, the flesh is then fried with nuts and spices and stuffed back into the skin. Baked or grilled (broiled), this stuffed fish is quite impressive and tends to be a speciality on restaurant menus in Istanbul.

Chunks of firm-fleshed fish are sometimes cooked in earthenware pots with vegetables, spices and herbs to make a regional stew, or they are marinated and threaded on kebab sticks and chargrilled. Gutted and cleaned, small anchovies and sardines are salted, dipped in flour and fried until golden brown on both sides, then served whole with dill and lemon.

Shellfish, squid and octopus are mainly enjoyed in Istanbul and the Aegean and Mediterranean towns. Prawns (shrimp) are stir-fried with garlic and cumin, or baked with peppers and onions in earthenware pots. Some restaurants offer prawn kebabs, or mixed fish kebabs with a few prawns thrown in, and prawns are also added to rice dishes. Whole mussels in their shells are stuffed with rice, a great favourite on the Istanbul and Izmir waterfronts, and they are cooked in a traditional *pilaki* dish that is generally served cold in a *meze* spread. Squid rings and mussels are deep-fried in batter and often served with a garlic-flavoured sauce, while baby squid are sometimes stuffed with aromatic rice and herbs, and octopus is usually grilled and tossed in a salad with olives and peppers.

Ancient methods of preserving fish are still adhered to. Small fish are gutted, split open and hung up on a line to dry, resembling a washing line of socks. Dried fish are generally reconstituted in soups, stocks and stews, sardines and anchovies are preserved whole in vinegar or brine, while pickled anchovies are popular on the Black Sea coast. Generally, though, fish is bought very fresh, straight off the boats at the daily fish market, where some of the smaller species are still swimming around in buckets,

while others are laid out on ice, with their bright eyes and gleaming skins. Sloshing about in their rubber boots, the fish sellers will help you select the fish for your chosen dish, then prepare it for you as you wait.

According to traditional Anatolian folklore, which draws from the story in the Koran of the table descending from heaven for Jesus Christ, there were two fishes and five loaves on that table. After 5,000 men, women and children had consumed as much as they possibly could, the quantity multiplied miraculously into 12 large baskets of fish and bread. For this reason, fish and bread symbolize fertility in the Muslim faith and they are always treated with great respect in Anatolia.

Although fish features in Anatolian folklore and anchovies are sung about on the Black Sea coast, the fish cuisine of Turkey is relatively recent. Early cookbooks provide few records of fish dishes, although the Ottoman period produced such delicacies as *uskumru dolması* and *midye dolması*, stuffed mussels. More contemporary cooks, on the other hand, have made creative use of the rich supply of seafood, a fact that is much in evidence in some of the fish restaurants along the Bosphorus and on the famous esplanade in Izmir.

Above, from left to right
swordfish, karides güveç, *sea bass*

chargrilled sardines in vine leaves

This is a popular summer dish made with small sardines freshly plucked from the sea. Although they can be cooked easily under a conventional grill, there is nothing to beat the aroma and taste when they are cooked over a charcoal barbecue in the open air – and the tangy, charred vine leaves and tomatoes make perfect partners for the oily flesh of the fish.

1 Put all the dressing ingredients in a bowl, season with salt and pepper and mix well.

2 Pat the sardines dry and lay them in a flat dish. Mix 30ml/2 tbsp oil with the lemon juice and brush over the sardines.

3 Get the barbecue ready for cooking. Meanwhile, spread the vine leaves out on a flat surface and place a sardine on each leaf. Sprinkle each one with a little salt and wrap loosely in the leaf like a cigar, with the tail and head poking out.

4 Brush each leaf with a little oil and place seam side down to keep them from unravelling. Thread the tomatoes on skewers and sprinkle with a little salt.

5 Cook the sardines and tomatoes on the barbecue for 2–3 minutes on each side, until the vine leaves are charred and the tomatoes are soft.

6 Transfer the vine leaves and tomatoes to a serving dish and drizzle with the dressing. Serve immediately, with lemon wedges for squeezing.

12 sardines, scaled, gutted and thoroughly washed

30ml/2 tbsp olive oil, plus extra for brushing

juice of ½ lemon

12 fresh or preserved vine leaves (see below)

4–6 vine tomatoes, halved or quartered

salt and ground black pepper

lemon wedges, to serve

FOR THE DRESSING

60ml/4 tbsp olive oil

juice of 1 lemon

15ml/1 tbsp balsamic or white wine vinegar

5–10ml/1–2 tsp clear honey

5ml/1 tsp Turkish red pepper, or 1 fresh red chilli, finely chopped

a few fresh dill fronds and flat leaf parsley sprigs, finely chopped

SERVES 3–4

preparing vine leaves *Fresh vine leaves are sold in Turkish markets, and you can get them in Middle Eastern and Mediterranean stores when they are in season in the autumn. Plunged into boiling water for a minute, the bright green leaves soften and turn a deep olive colour, ready for use. If you can't get fresh vine leaves, you can use the ones preserved in brine that are available in packets at supermarkets and delicatessens. They require soaking in water to remove the salt. Place them in a bowl, pour boiling water over them and leave to soak for about an hour. Drain and rinse under cold running water, then pat dry.*

per portion Energy 300kcal/1245kJ; Protein 16.5g; Carbohydrate 5.3g, of which sugars 5.3g; Fat 23.7g, of which saturates 4.5g; Cholesterol 0mg; Calcium 82mg; Fibre 1.5g; Sodium 101mg.

baked sardines with tomatoes, thyme and purple basil

With the hillsides covered in herbs, aromatic fish dishes like this one are a common feature of the Aegean and Mediterranean coasts. Purple basil, which has a mild aniseed taste, is used frequently, although green holy basil and lemon basil work just as well.

1 Preheat the oven to 180°C/350°F/ Gas 4. Lay the sardines side by side in an ovenproof dish, place a sprig of thyme between each one and squeeze the lemon juice over them.

2 In a bowl, mix the tomatoes, olive oil, garlic and sugar. Season and stir in most of the basil leaves, then tip the mixture over the sardines. Bake, uncovered, for 25 minutes. Sprinkle the remaining basil leaves over the top and serve hot, with lemon wedges.

8 large sardines, scaled, gutted and thoroughly washed

6–8 fresh thyme sprigs

juice of ½ lemon

2 x 400g/14oz cans chopped tomatoes, drained of juice

60–75ml/4–5 tbsp olive oil

4 garlic cloves, smashed flat

5ml/1 tsp sugar

1 bunch of fresh purple basil

salt and ground black pepper

lemon wedges, to serve

SERVES 4

per portion Energy 219kcal/915kJ; Protein 11.7g; Carbohydrate 7.3g, of which sugars 7.3g; Fat 16.2g, of which saturates 3.1g; Cholesterol 0mg; Calcium 57mg; Fibre 2g; Sodium 78mg.

kiliç şiş

Any firm-fleshed fish, such as tuna, trout, salmon, monkfish or sea bass, can be used for kebabs, but the classic *kiliç şiş* made with meaty chunks of swordfish is a firm favourite in restaurants. Usually served as a main course with a rocket and herb salad, they are light and tasty.

500g/1¼lb boneless swordfish loin or steaks, cut into bitesize chunks

1 lemon, halved lengthways and sliced

1 large tomato, halved, seeded and cut into bitesize pieces

2 hot green peppers (see below) or 1 green (bell) pepper, seeded and cut into bitesize pieces

a handful of bay leaves

lemon wedges, to serve

FOR THE MARINADE

1 onion, grated

1–2 garlic cloves, crushed

juice of ½ lemon

30–45ml/2–3 tbsp olive oil

5–10ml/1–2 tsp tomato purée (paste)

salt and ground black pepper

SERVES 4

1 Mix the marinade ingredients in a shallow bowl. Toss in the chunks of swordfish and set aside for about 30 minutes.

2 Thread the fish on to skewers, alternating with the lemon, tomato and peppers and the occasional bay leaf. If there is any marinade left, brush it over the kebabs.

3 Put a cast-iron griddle pan over a medium heat until very hot. Place the skewers on the pan and cook for 2–3 minutes on each side until the kebab ingredients are quite charred.

4 Serve the kebabs hot with lemon wedges for squeezing.

hot green peppers *In Turkish these peppers are called çarliston biber. They are light green, and shaped like Turkish slippers. Most çarliston biber are sweet, and mainly used raw in meze and salads, but some have a hint of heat and are good for cooked dishes like the kebabs here. Look out for them in Turkish and Middle Eastern stores.*

per portion Energy 225kcal/940kJ; Protein 23.9g; Carbohydrate 7.8g, of which sugars 7.2g; Fat 11.1g, of which saturates 2g; Cholesterol 51mg; Calcium 18mg; Fibre 1.9g; Sodium 177mg.

mackerel pilaki

2 good-sized fresh mackerel, gutted and rinsed

120ml/4fl oz/½ cup olive oil

2 onions, chopped

3–4 garlic cloves, chopped

1 mild fresh green chilli, seeded and chopped

2–3 carrots, diced

2–3 potatoes, diced

1 medium celeriac, weighing about 450g/1lb, peeled, trimmed and diced

2 large tomatoes, skinned and chopped, or 400g/14oz can chopped tomatoes, drained of juice

5ml/1 tsp sugar

2–3 bay leaves

juice of 2 lemons

1 small bunch of fresh flat leaf parsley

salt and ground black pepper

SERVES 4–6

Pilaki dishes all follow the same cooking method, whether made with meaty beans, fish or shellfish. In Istanbul there is a popular *pilaki* made with mussels, but the most common *pilaki* are made with good-sized, firm-fleshed fish. The classic one is made with bonito, but mackerel and sea bass are equally good.

1 Preheat the oven to 170°C/325°F/ Gas 3. Using a sharp knife, cut the fish crossways into 2cm/¾in slices, keeping it intact at the backbone.

2 Heat the oil in a heavy pan. Stir in the onions, garlic and chilli and cook until soft. Add the carrots, potatoes and celeriac and cook for 1–2 minutes, then stir in the tomatoes, sugar and bay leaves.

3 Pour in 600ml/1 pint/2½ cups water and bring to the boil. Lower the heat, cover the pan and simmer for 5–10 minutes, until the vegetables are tender but not mushy. Season with salt and pepper.

4 Spoon half the vegetables over the bottom of an ovenproof dish, place the fish on top and spoon the remaining vegetables over them. Sprinkle with the lemon juice and lay a few sprigs of parsley on top.

5 Cover with baking parchment that has been soaked in water and squeezed out, then place in the oven for 20 minutes, or until the fish is cooked.

6 Remove the paper and parsley sprigs and serve hot, garnished with a little roughly chopped parsley. Alternatively, leave the *pilaki* to cool in the dish and serve at room temperature.

per portion Energy 270kcal/1127kJ; Protein 17.3g; Carbohydrate 22.9g, of which sugars 11.2g; Fat 12.7g, of which saturates 2.7g; Cholesterol 40mg; Calcium 76mg; Fibre 4.1g; Sodium 115mg.

1.2kg/2½lb very fresh sea bass (see below), gutted, with head and tail left on

about 1kg/2¼lb coarse sea salt

ground black pepper and lemon wedges, to serve

SERVES 2–4

sea bass baked in salt

This is a restaurant speciality, especially popular along the Bosphorus in Istanbul and the waterfront restaurants in Izmir. A good-sized fish, completely masked in sea salt, is baked until the salt is as hard as rock. It is then transported to the eager diners by proud waiters, who crack open the salt casing with a heavy mallet and remove the top layer of skin to reveal the bleached white flesh of the cooked fish beneath. This ancient method of cooking intensifies the freshness of the fish, conjuring up the taste of the sea, but it does require a lot of salt. For supreme enjoyment, little else is needed – sauces would disguise the freshness. Serve on its own with lemon, freshly ground black pepper and a rocket salad.

suitable types of fish *In Turkey, bluefish is popular for this dish, but if you are unable to get it sea bass is an acceptable alternative. You could equally well use any other firm-fleshed white fish, such as turbot or sole.*

1 Preheat the oven to 190°C/375°F/ Gas 5. Rinse the fish inside and out. Find an ovenproof dish to fit the fish and cover the bottom with a thick layer of salt, pressing it down with the heel of your hand. Place the fish on top and shovel spoonfuls of salt over it until it is completely covered, then press down gently to compact it. Put the dish in the oven and bake for 1 hour, until the salt has formed a hard crust.

2 Place the dish on the table and crack open the salt crust with a heavy object, such as a meat cleaver or a pestle. Carefully peel off the top layer of salt, removing the skin of the fish with it. Serve chunks of the delicate white flesh immediately, with nothing more than a little black pepper and a squeeze of lemon.

per portion Energy 175kcal/737kJ; Protein 33.8g; Carbohydrate 0g, of which sugars 0g; Fat 4.4g, of which saturates 0.7g; Cholesterol 140mg; Calcium 228mg; Fibre 0g; Sodium 1103mg.

450g/1lb skinless fresh white fish fillets, such as haddock or sea bass

2 slices of day-old bread, sprinkled with water and left for a few minutes, then squeezed dry

1 red onion, finely chopped

30ml/2 tbsp currants, soaked in warm water for 5–10 minutes and drained

30ml/2 tbsp pine nuts

1 small bunch each of fresh flat leaf parsley, mint and dill, finely chopped

1 egg

5–10ml/1–2 tsp tomato purée (paste) or ketchup

15ml/1 tbsp ground cinnamon

45–60ml/3–4 tbsp plain (all-purpose) flour

45–60ml/3–4 tbsp sunflower oil

salt and ground black pepper

TO SERVE

1 small bunch of fresh flat leaf parsley

1–2 lemons or limes, cut into wedges

SERVES 4

cinnamon fishcakes with currants, pine nuts and herbs

Whether served as a hot *meze* or as a main course with a salad, these fresh, tasty fishcakes are delicious flavoured with cinnamon and the ubiquitous triad of herbs – parsley, mint and dill.

1 In a bowl, break up the fish with a fork. Add the bread, onion, currants and pine nuts, toss in the herbs and mix well.

2 In another small bowl, beat the egg with the tomato purée and 10ml/2 tsp of the cinnamon. Pour the mixture over the fish and season with salt and pepper, then mix with your hands and mould into small balls.

3 Mix the flour on a plate with the remaining cinnamon. Press each ball into a flat cake and coat in the flour.

4 Heat the oil in a wide, shallow pan and fry the fishcakes in batches for 8–10 minutes, until golden brown. Lift out and drain on kitchen paper. Serve hot on a bed of parsley, with lemon or lime wedges for squeezing.

per portion Energy 317kcal/1324kJ; Protein 26.1g; Carbohydrate 17.8g, of which sugars 2.5g; Fat 16.2g, of which saturates 1.9g; Cholesterol 99mg; Calcium 79mg; Fibre 1.6g; Sodium 169mg.

uskumru dolması

This dish of whole mackerel stuffed with nuts and spices is an Ottoman classic. One of Istanbul's most inspired dishes, the fish is skilfully massaged to empty it of flesh while keeping the skin intact, so that it can be stuffed to resemble the whole fish once more.

1 large, fresh mackerel, scaled and thoroughly washed, but not gutted

30–45ml/2–3 tbsp olive oil

4–5 shallots, finely chopped

30ml/2 tbsp pine nuts

30ml/2 tbsp blanched almonds, finely slivered

45ml/3 tbsp walnuts, finely chopped

15–30ml/1–2 tbsp currants, soaked in warm water for 5–10 minutes and drained

6–8 dried apricots, finely chopped

5–10ml/1–2 tsp ground cinnamon

5ml/1 tsp ground allspice

2.5ml/½ tsp ground cloves

5ml/1 tsp Turkish red pepper or 2.5ml/½ tsp chilli powder

5ml/1 tsp sugar

1 small bunch each of fresh flat leaf parsley and dill, finely chopped

juice of 1 lemon

plain (all-purpose) flour

sunflower oil, for shallow frying

salt and ground black pepper

TO SERVE

1 bunch of fresh dill

a few fresh flat leaf parsley sprigs

1 lemon, cut into wedges

SERVES 4

1 Take a sharp knife and cut an opening just below the gills of the mackerel, making sure the head and backbone remain intact. Push your finger into the opening and remove the guts, then rinse the fish inside and out.

2 Using a rolling pin or mallet, gently bash the fish on both sides, making sure you smash the backbone. Now, with your hands, gently massage the skin to loosen it away from the flesh – don't pummel it too hard or the skin will tear.

3 Working from the tail end towards the head, squeeze the loosened flesh out of the opening below the gills – use a similar motion to squeezing a half-empty tube of toothpaste. Remove any bits of bone from the loosened flesh, then rinse out the mackerel sack and set aside.

4 Heat the oil in a frying pan, stir in the shallots and cook until soft. Add the nuts and stir until they begin to colour. Add the currants, apricots, spices, red pepper or chilli and sugar. Mix in the fish flesh and cook through for 2–3 minutes, then toss in the herbs and lemon juice and season with salt and pepper.

5 Lift up the empty mackerel skin and push the filling through the opening, shaking the sack a little to jiggle the filling down towards the tail.

6 As the skin begins to fill, gently squeeze the mixture downwards to make it compact, until it looks like a plump, fresh mackerel once more.

7 To cook the mackerel, toss it in flour and fry in sunflower oil, or brush with a little oil and grill (broil) until the skin begins to turn brown and buckle.

8 To serve, cut the fish crossways into thick slices and arrange on a dish in the shape of the fish. Surround with dill and parsley and serve with lemon wedges.

per portion Energy 520Kcal/2154kJ; Protein 20.2g; Carbohydrate 13.7g, of which sugars 10.1g; Fat 43.1g, of which saturates 5.5g; Cholesterol 40mg; Calcium 86mg; Fibre 3.1g; Sodium 53mg.

Mediterranean squid with olives and red wine

Although many Muslims are non-drinkers, there are some surprisingly good wines in Turkey, and along the Mediterranean and Aegean coasts some restaurants incorporate wine in dishes. This could be due to their proximity to Greece or, perhaps, to the influence of Western tourists.

1 Heat the oil in a heavy pan and cook the onions and garlic until golden.

2 Add the squid heads and rings and toss them in the pan for 2–3 minutes, until they begin to colour. Toss in the olives, cinnamon and sugar, pour in the wine and add the bay leaves.

3 Bubble up the liquid, then lower the heat and cover the pan. Cook gently for 35–40 minutes, until most of the liquid has reduced and the squid is tender.

4 Season the squid with salt and pepper and toss in the herbs. Serve immediately, with lemon wedges.

30–45ml/2–3 tbsp olive oil

2 red onions, cut in half lengthways and sliced along the grain

3–4 garlic cloves, chopped

about 750g/1lb 10oz fresh squid, prepared as below, cut into thick rings

45–60ml/3–4 tbsp black olives, pitted

5–10ml/1–2 tsp ground cinnamon

5–10ml/1–2 tsp sugar

about 300ml/½ pint/1¼ cups red wine

2 bay leaves

1 small bunch each of fresh flat leaf parsley and dill, finely chopped

salt and ground black pepper

lemon wedges, to serve

SERVES 4

preparing squid *Fresh squid should smell slightly sweet. Rinse it and peel off the thin film of skin, then sever the head and trim the tentacles with a sharp knife. With your finger, pull out the backbone and reach down into the body pouch to remove the ink sac and any mushy bits. Rinse the empty pouch inside and out and pat dry. Use the pouch and trimmed head for cooking; discard the rest.*

per portion Energy 304kcal/1275kJ; Protein 30.3g; Carbohydrate 11.4g, of which sugars 6.8g; Fat 10.1g, of which saturates 1.7g; Cholesterol 422mg; Calcium 62mg; Fibre 1.7g, Sodium 468mg.

karides güveç

This popular prawn dish is often served as hot *meze* in the fish restaurants of Izmir and Istanbul. The Mediterranean version, found in the coastal regions of south-west Turkey, is flavoured with a dose of garlic, red pepper and coriander seeds. Cooked in one big earthenware pot, *güveç*, or in small individual ones as here, it is delicious served with a green salad.

30–45ml/2–3 tbsp olive oil

1 onion, cut in half lengthways and finely sliced along the grain

1 green (bell) pepper, seeded and finely sliced

2–3 garlic cloves, chopped

5–10ml/1–2 tsp coriander seeds

5–10ml/1–2 tsp Turkish red pepper, or 1 fresh red chilli, seeded and chopped

5–10ml/1–2 tsp sugar

splash of white wine vinegar

2 x 400g/14oz cans chopped tomatoes

1 small bunch of fresh flat leaf parsley, chopped

500g/1¼lb fresh raw prawns (shrimp), shelled, thoroughly cleaned and drained

about 120g/4oz *kasar peyniri*, Parmesan or a strong dry Cheddar, grated

salt and ground black pepper

SERVES 4

1 Heat the oil in a heavy pan, stir in the onion, green pepper, garlic, coriander seeds and red pepper or chilli and cook until they begin to colour. Stir in the sugar, vinegar, tomatoes and parsley, then cook gently for about 25 minutes, until you have a chunky sauce. While the sauce is cooking, preheat the oven to 200°C/400°F/Gas 6.

2 Season the sauce with salt and pepper and toss in the prawns, making sure they are mixed in well.

3 Spoon the mixture into individual earthenware pots and sprinkle the top with the grated cheese. Bake for 25 minutes, or until the cheese is nicely browned on top.

per portion Energy 338kcal/1413kJ; Protein 35.9g; Carbohydrate 11.2g, of which sugars 10.8g; Fat 16.9g, of which saturates 7.3g; Cholesterol 274mg; Calcium 481mg; Fibre 2.9g; Sodium 585mg.

mussels stuffed with aromatic pilaff and pine nuts

In Istanbul, stuffed mussels are sold by street vendors around the Golden Horn, at the boat crossings over the Bosphorus, and in the main bazaars. In the fish restaurants, they are always served at room temperature as a popular *meze* dish.

16 large fresh mussels

45–60ml/3–4 tbsp olive oil

2–3 shallots, finely chopped

30ml/2 tbsp pine nuts

30ml/2 tbsp currants, soaked in warm water for 5–10 minutes and drained

10ml/2 tsp ground cinnamon

5ml/1 tsp ground allspice

5–10ml/1–2 tsp sugar

5–10ml/1–2 tsp tomato purée (paste)

115g/4oz/generous ½ cup short grain or pudding rice, well rinsed and drained

1 small bunch each of fresh flat leaf parsley, mint and dill, finely chopped

salt and ground black pepper

lemon wedges and fresh flat leaf parsley sprigs, to serve

SERVES 4

cleaning mussels *Place the mussels in a bowl of cold water and scrub the shells with a stiff brush. Pull out the tough beards and cut off the barnacles with a knife. Discard any mussels that are open, or that do not close when tapped on the work surface.*

1 Clean the mussels as described below. Keep them in a bowl of cold water while you prepare the stuffing.

2 Heat the oil in a heavy pan, stir in the shallots and cook until they soften. Add the pine nuts and currants, stir for 1–2 minutes until the pine nuts turn golden and the currants plump up, then stir in the cinnamon, allspice, sugar and tomato purée. Now add the rice, and stir until it is well coated.

3 Pour in enough water to just cover the rice. Season with salt and pepper and bring to the boil. Lower the heat, partially cover the pan and simmer for 10–12 minutes, until all the water has been absorbed. Tip the rice on to a plate, leave to cool, then toss in the herbs.

4 Using a sharp knife, prise open each mussel shell wide enough to fill with rice. Stuff a spoonful of rice into each shell, then close the shells and pack the mussels tightly into a steamer filled with water. Cover with a sheet of dampened baking parchment, put a plate on top and weigh it down with a stone – one from the garden will do – to prevent the mussels from opening during steaming.

5 Place the lid on the steamer and bring the water to the boil. Lower the heat and steam the mussels gently for 15–20 minutes, then leave to cool a little in the pan.

6 Serve warm on a bed of parsley, with lemon wedges for squeezing.

per portion Energy 319kcal/1328kJ; Protein 13.3g; Carbohydrate 32.7g, of which sugars 7.5g; Fat 15g, of which saturates 1.9g; Cholesterol 33mg; Calcium 49mg; Fibre 0.5g; Sodium 237mg.

MEAT AND POULTRY

çöp şiş

Arnavut ciğeri

meatballs with pine nuts and cinnamon

vine leaves stuffed with lamb and rice

yoğurtlu şiş kebab

lamb cutlets with tomato sauce

chargrilled quails in pomegranate marinade

chicken casserole with okra and lemon

Çerkez tavuğu

lemon chicken thighs wrapped in aubergine

meat and poultry

The enticing smell of spicy chicken and lamb kebabs grilling in the streets and kebab houses is very much a feature of the intricate culinary aroma that wafts around Turkey.

Ever since the early Turks of central Asia herded sheep to new grazing grounds, lamb and mutton have been an integral part of the Turkish diet. The fat-tailed sheep are the most highly prized, because they also provide many Anatolian Turks with their favourite cooking fat. Cattle were raised for producing milk and tilling the fields in the early history of Anatolia, so beef was rarely eaten, but in modern-day Turkey beef is available for those who can afford it, often cooked in stews and minced (ground) for fillings and *köfte* (meatballs) in place of lamb. Wild game, such as rabbit, deer and bear, featured in the diet of the early hunters and was also sought after by Ottoman sultans, but today it rarely turns up on the Turkish table.

Once Islam had taken root in Anatolia, the dietary laws laid out in the Koran enforced fasting and feasting on holy days, as well as restrictions on the intake of alcohol and the handling and eating of meat. The Koran commands that an animal must be slaughtered by cutting its throat, that the blood must not be consumed, and that any form of pork is forbidden.

The month of fasting between sunrise and sunset, *Ramazan*, and the holy festival, *Kurban Bayramı*, which marks the near sacrifice of Isaac, are important events for devout Muslims. At *Kurban Bayramı*, sheep are herded through streets, villages and markets, where families gather to buy one to take home and sacrifice. The family then chooses the cuts of meat and offal they want, giving the rest to the poor people in the neighbourhood. Special dishes made at this time include *işkembe çorbası*, the traditional tripe soup; *kavurma*, which involves frying the meat in its own fat; *kıkırdak poğaçası*, a delicacy made by boiling the fat tail; and *bumbar dolması*, a dish of grilled (broiled) intestines stuffed with liver, onions, spices and currants, of which there is a similar street version, *kokoreç*.

Outside the country, *döner* and *şiş* kebabs are perhaps the best-known of Turkish meat dishes, but in Turkey itself kebabs come in many other guises – some grilled or roasted, others baked in paper or in earthenware pots. Many popular kebabs are served on *pide* with a yogurt or tomato sauce, while the fiery kebabs from the *güney* kitchen in the south of Turkey are often

Above, from left to right
Lamb cutlets, stuffed vine leaves, Arnavut ciğeri.

made of minced meat and plenty of Turkish red pepper. Other notable dishes that are made with minced meat include *ali nazık*, aubergine (eggplant) purée layered with minced meat and yogurt; *karnıyarık,* the famous "split belly" from the Palace kitchens made from aubergines stuffed with minced meat; and the numerous different *köfte*, including the Ottoman *kadın buduğu* (ladies' thighs).

Sautéing is a popular cooking method for meat, and so too is stewing – as in the traditional *yahni*, a stew of meat and onions. Then there are the Anatolian *güveç* dishes cooked in earthenware pots or curved roof tiles, which produce moist mixtures of meat and vegetables or pulses. Traditional spit-roasting is reserved for special occasions, as it requires the digging of a pit in the ground in which a whole lamb or goat, rubbed with salt and spices, is cooked slowly over the glowing embers to produce exceptionally tasty meat.

In the Anatolian villages, large cuts of meat are usually cooked in a communal *tandır* (clay oven), but for small cuts of meat and chicken everyone in Turkey has a *mangal*, a small charcoal stove for outdoor cooking that can be conveniently set up on a city balcony or transported to the beach or woods for a picnic.

Spit-roasting is also popular in Anatolia. A deep pit, which must be big enough to contain one or two whole lambs or goats, is dug by hand, lined with fire bricks, and a wood fire is lit at the bottom. When the embers are red hot the animals, which have been well rubbed with salt and spices, are hung over the pit suspended from a hook. Covered with a iron lid and sealed with clay, the meat is left to cook in the pit for at least three hours until it is beautifully moist and tender.

Chicken is undoubtedly the most popular kind of poultry in Turkey, and it is eaten almost as often as lamb. Medieval recipes include lavish dishes of duck stuffed with olives and figs, and even quails stuffed with aubergines, but neither of these birds makes frequent appearances on modern menus. Chicken is cooked in many different ways – spit-roasted, used for kebabs and *köfte*, stewed with vegetables, and stuffed with apricots and roasted.

One of the best chicken dishes of all is *çerkez tavuğu*, a recipe that originated in Circassia and is now very much part of modern Turkish cuisine. Some Anatolian versions of the dish include coriander (cilantro), but the Istanbul version topped with melted butter and Turkish red pepper is especially delicious.

Above, from left to right
Köfte, *meatballs with pine nuts and cinnamon,* şiş kebab.

çöp şiş

This popular Anatolian kebab is traditionally made with lamb scraps – *çöp* means rubbish – that are chargrilled on swords. The small pieces of cooked meat are then wrapped in freshly griddled flat bread with red onion, flat leaf parsley and a squeeze of lemon.

2 onions

7.5ml/1½ tsp salt

2 garlic cloves, crushed

10ml/2 tsp cumin seeds, crushed

900g/2lb boneless shoulder of lamb, trimmed and cut into bitesize pieces

FOR THE FLAT BREADS

225g/8oz/2 cups strong white bread flour

50g/2oz/¼ cup wholemeal (whole-wheat) flour

5ml/1 tsp salt

TO SERVE

1 large red onion, cut in half lengthways, in half again crossways, and sliced along the grain

1 large bunch of fresh flat leaf parsley, roughly chopped

2–3 lemons, cut into wedges

SERVES 4–6

1 Grate the onions on to a plate, sprinkle with the salt and leave them to weep for about 15 minutes. Place a sieve (strainer) over a large bowl, tip in the onions and press down with the back of a wooden spoon to extract the juice. Discard the onions left in the sieve, then mix the garlic and cumin seeds into the onion juice and toss in the lamb. Cover and leave to marinate for 3–4 hours.

2 Meanwhile, prepare the dough for the breads. Sift the flours and salt into a bowl. Make a well in the middle and gradually add 200ml/7fl oz/scant 1 cup lukewarm water, drawing in the flour from the sides. Using your hands, knead the dough until firm and springy – if the dough is at all sticky, add more flour.

3 Divide the dough into 24 pieces and knead each one into a ball. Place on a floured surface and cover with a damp cloth. Leave to rest for 45 minutes while you get the barbecue ready.

4 Just before cooking, roll each ball of dough into a wide, thin circle. Dust them with flour so they don't stick together, and keep them covered with a damp dish towel to prevent them drying out.

5 Thread the meat on to flat kebab swords or metal skewers and cook on the barbecue for 2–3 minutes on each side. At the same time, cook the flat breads on a hot griddle or other flat pan, flipping them over as they begin to go brown and buckle. Pile up on a plate.

6 When the kebabs are cooked, slide the meat off the skewers on to the flat breads. Sprinkle onion and parsley over each pile and squeeze lemon juice over the top. Wrap the breads into parcels and eat with your hands.

per portion Energy 433kcal/1821kJ; Protein 34.3g; Carbohydrate 37.1g, of which sugars 4.4g; Fat 17.5g, of which saturates 7.9g; Cholesterol 114mg; Calcium 83mg; Fibre 2.5g; Sodium 460mg.

Arnavut ciğeri

This is such a delicious way to eat lamb's liver that it is even possible to convert those who don't usually like it. Translated as "Albanian liver", it is one of those dishes that was adopted by the Palace kitchens as the Ottoman Empire consumed vast expanses of Eastern Europe. Traditionally served as a hot or cold *meze* dish with sliced red onion and flat leaf parsley, it is also a wonderful dish for supper, served with a salad and a dollop of creamy yogurt if you like.

500g/1¼lb fresh lamb's liver

30ml/2 tbsp plain (all-purpose) flour

5–10ml/1–2 tsp Turkish red pepper or paprika

45–60ml/3–4 tbsp olive oil

2 garlic cloves, finely chopped

5–10ml/1–2 tsp cumin seeds

sea salt

1 large red onion, cut in half lengthways, in half again crossways, and sliced along the grain

TO SERVE

a handful of fresh flat leaf parsley

1 lemon, cut into wedges

SERVES 4

1 Place the liver on a chopping board. Using a sharp knife, remove any skin and ducts, then cut the liver into thin strips or bitesize cubes.

2 Mix the flour and red pepper or paprika in a shallow bowl and toss the liver in it until well coated.

3 Heat the oil in a heavy pan. Add the garlic and cumin seeds, season with sea salt and cook until the cumin gives off a nutty aroma. Toss in the liver and stir-fry quickly for 2–3 minutes so that it cooks on all sides. Remove and drain on kichen paper.

4 Spread the sliced onion on a serving dish, spoon the the liver in the middle and garnish with parsley leaves. Serve hot or cold, with the lemon wedges for squeezing.

per portion Energy 298kcal/1245kJ; Protein 27g; Carbohydrate 11.8g, of which sugars 4.3g; Fat 16.3g, of which saturates 3.3g; Cholesterol 538mg; Calcium 37mg; Fibre 1.3g; Sodium 94mg.

meatballs with pine nuts and cinnamon

There are a number of different types of meatball in the Turkish kitchen. Falling under the generic name *köfte*, they are generally made from lamb or beef, although some contain chicken, and they are shaped into round balls or plump ovals.

250g/9oz/generous 1 cup lean minced (ground) lamb

1 onion, finely chopped

2 garlic cloves, crushed

10–15ml/2–3 tsp ground cinnamon

30ml/2 tbsp pine nuts

30ml/2 tbsp currants, soaked in warm water for 5–10 minutes and drained

5ml/1 tsp Turkish red pepper or paprika

2 slices of day-old white or brown bread, ground into crumbs

1 egg, lightly beaten

15ml/1 tbsp tomato ketchup

1 bunch each of fresh flat leaf parsley and dill

60ml/4 tbsp plain (all-purpose) flour

sunflower oil, for shallow frying

salt and ground black pepper

lemon wedges, to serve

SERVES 4–6

meatballs to go *Omit the currants and pine nuts and add 5ml/1 tsp ground cumin and 1 chopped fresh hot chilli. Shape into small balls, cook as above for 5–6 minutes, then tuck into toasted pitta bread pockets with sliced red onion, chopped flat leaf parsley and garlic-flavoured yogurt.*

1 In a bowl, pound the lamb with the onion, garlic and cinnamon. Knead with your hands and knock out the air, then add the pine nuts with the currants, red pepper or paprika, breadcrumbs, egg and ketchup. Season with salt and pepper.

2 Finely chop the herbs, reserving 1–2 sprigs of parsley for the garnish, and knead into the mixture, making sure all the ingredients are mixed well together.

3 Take apricot-size portions of the mixture in your hands and roll into balls. Flatten each ball so that it resembles a thick disc, then coat lightly in the flour.

4 Heat a thin layer of oil in a heavy pan. Add the meatballs and cook for 8–10 minutes, until browned on all sides. Remove with a slotted spoon and drain on kitchen paper. Serve hot with lemon wedges and garnish with parsley.

per portion Energy 261kcal/1088kJ; Protein 11.4g; Carbohydrate 15.4g, of which sugars 5.2g; Fat 17.5g, of which saturates 4g; Cholesterol 64mg; Calcium 40mg; Fibre 0.7g; Sodium 129mg.

vine leaves stuffed with lamb and rice

Vine leaves are generally used for wrapping around fish or cheese, or for stuffing and rolling into logs. The best known stuffed vine leaves are the ones filled with aromatic rice and served cold. In Turkish, these are known as *yalancı yaprak dolması*, meaning false stuffed vine leaves, because they do not contain meat. The meat-filled version, *etli yaprak dolması*, is regarded as the real thing, and is usually served hot as a main course with a dollop of yogurt.

350g/12oz/1½ cups finely minced (ground) lean lamb or beef

2 onions, finely chopped

115g/4oz/generous ½ cup long grain rice, thoroughly rinsed and drained

1 bunch each of fresh dill, flat leaf parsley and mint, finely chopped

45–60ml/3–4 tbsp olive oil

25–30 fresh or preserved vine leaves

juice of 1 lemon

salt and ground black pepper

TO SERVE

60–90ml/4–6 tbsp thick and creamy natural (plain) yogurt

1 lemon, cut into wedges

SERVES 4–6

1 Put the lamb in a bowl and stir in the onions, rice and herbs. Season with salt and pepper, bind with 15ml/1 tbsp of the oil and knead with your hands.

2 Lay one of the vine leaves on a flat surface and spoon a little of the meat and rice mixture at the top of the leaf. Pull the top of the leaf over the filling, fold in the sides, then roll the leaf into a tight, stout-shaped log. Repeat with the remaining leaves and filling.

3 Arrange the stuffed vine leaves, seam side down, in a deep, wide, heavy pan. Pack them tightly together in circles, making more than one layer if they won't all fit on the bottom of the pan.

4 In a bowl, mix the remaining oil with the lemon juice and 150ml/¼ pint/⅔ cup water, then pour over the vine leaves. The liquid should come at least halfway up the top layer, so you may need to add extra liquid.

5 Put the pan over a medium heat. Once the liquid begins to bubble, place a plate over the leaves to stop them from unravelling, followed by a lid or foil. Lower the heat and leave the vine leaves to steam gently for 45 minutes, until the rice and meat are cooked. Serve hot, with the yogurt and lemon wedges.

per portion Energy 276kcal/1148kJ; Protein 14.6g; Carbohydrate 23.5g, of which sugars 6.6g; Fat 13.8g, of which saturates 4.4g; Cholesterol 45mg; Calcium 88mg; Fibre 2.8g; Sodium 51mg.

yoğurtlu şiş kebab

This is the ultimate kebab – chargrilled meat served on flat bread with yogurt and tomatoes. Designed to use up day-old *pide*, for which you can substitute pitta bread or a plain Indian naan, the dish is succulent and tasty, and should be devoured on its own.

12 plum tomatoes

30ml/2 tbsp butter

1 large *pide*, or 4 pitta or small naan, cut into bitesize chunks

5ml/1 tsp ground *sumac*

5ml/1 tsp dried oregano

225g/8oz/1 cup thick and creamy natural (plain) yogurt

salt and ground black pepper

1 bunch of fresh flat leaf parsley, chopped, to garnish

FOR THE KEBABS

500g/1¼lb/2¼ cups lean minced (ground) lamb

2 onions, finely chopped

1 fresh green chilli, seeded and finely chopped

4 garlic cloves, crushed

5ml/1 tsp Turkish red pepper or paprika

5ml/1 tsp ground *sumac*

1 bunch of fresh flat leaf parsley, finely chopped

FOR THE SAUCE

30ml/2 tbsp olive oil

15ml/1 tbsp butter

1 onion, finely chopped

2 garlic cloves, finely chopped

1 fresh green chilli, seeded and finely chopped

5–10ml/1–2 tsp sugar

400g/14oz can chopped tomatoes

SERVES 4

1 Make the kebabs. Put the lamb into a bowl with all the other ingredients and knead well to a smooth paste that is quite sticky. Cover and chill in the refrigerator for about 15 minutes.

2 Meanwhile, make the sauce. Heat the oil and butter in a heavy pan, stir in the onion, garlic and chilli and cook until they begin to colour. Add the sugar and tomatoes and cook, uncovered, for about 30 minutes until quite thick and saucy. Season with salt and pepper, remove from the heat and keep warm.

3 Get the barbecue ready for cooking and shape the kebabs. As soon as the kebabs are shaped, put them on the barbecue and cook for 6–8 minutes, turning once. Meanwhile, thread the whole plum tomatoes on to four skewers and place them on the barbecue until they are charred.

4 While the kebabs are cooking, melt the butter in a heavy pan and toss in the *pide* or other bread until golden. Sprinkle with some of the *sumac* and oregano, then arrange on a serving dish, spreading the pieces out so they form a flat base.

5 Splash a little sauce over the *pide* – not too much or it will go soggy – and spoon half the yogurt on top.

6 When the kebabs are cooked on both sides, slip the meat off the skewers and cut it into bitesize pieces. Arrange the meat on the *pide* with the tomatoes, sprinkle with salt and the rest of the *sumac* and oregano, and garnish with the chopped parsley.

7 Serve hot, topped with dollops of the remaining sauce and yogurt.

per portion Energy 642kcal/2688kJ; Protein 35.2g; Carbohydrate 52.8g, of which sugars 24.1g; Fat 33.9g, of which saturates 15.1g; Cholesterol 121mg; Calcium 253mg; Fibre 6.3g; Sodium 456mg.

lamb cutlets with tomato sauce

Lamb cutlets are more readily available, but veal is often favoured by the wealthier inhabitants of Ankara and Istanbul. Butchers prepare very fine cutlets by bashing them flat with a heavy meat cleaver. The cutlets are then quickly cooked on a griddle in their own fat, or a little butter, and served with a sprinkling of dried oregano and wedges of lemon, or with a piquant tomato sauce.

30ml/2 tbsp olive oil

10ml/2 tsp butter

12 lamb cutlets, trimmed and flattened with a cleaver – ask your butcher to do this

1 onion, finely chopped

1 fresh green chilli, seeded and finely chopped

2 garlic cloves, finely chopped

5ml/1 tsp sugar

5–10ml/1–2 tsp white wine vinegar

2–3 large tomatoes, skinned and chopped, or 400g/14oz can chopped tomatoes

1 green (bell) pepper, seeded and finely chopped

a sprinkling of dried oregano

salt and ground black pepper

SERVES 4

1 Heat the oil and butter in a large, heavy pan and quickly brown the cutlets on both sides. Remove the cutlets from the pan, add the onion, chilli and garlic, and fry until the onion begins to brown.

2 Stir in the sugar and vinegar, then add the tomatoes and green pepper. Lower the heat, cover and simmer for about 30 minutes, until the mixture is thick and saucy. Season with salt and pepper.

3 Return the cutlets to the pan, covering them in the sauce. Cook for about 15 minutes, until the meat is tender.

4 Transfer the cutlets to a serving dish, arranging them around the edge with the bones sticking outwards. Sprinkle with oregano, spoon the sauce in the middle and serve immediately.

per portion Energy 683kcal/2822kJ; Protein 23.2g; Carbohydrate 7.4g, of which sugars 6.9g; Fat 62.4g, of which saturates 29.2g; Cholesterol 122mg; Calcium 24mg; Fibre 1.7g; Sodium 114mg.

chargrilled quails in pomegranate marinade

This is a simple and tasty way of serving small birds, such as quails, poussins or grouse. The sharp marinade tenderizes the meat, as well as enhancing its flavour. In the Turkish countryside the quails are tucked into half a loaf of bread with onions, parsley and yogurt. Served straight off the charcoal grill with warm flat bread and a crunchy salad, they are delicious for lunch or supper.

4 quails, cleaned and boned
– ask your butcher to do this

juice of 4 pomegranates (see page 48)

juice of 1 lemon

30ml/2 tbsp olive oil

5–10ml/1–2 tsp Turkish red pepper,
or 5ml/1 tsp chilli powder

30–45ml/2–3 tbsp thick and creamy
natural (plain) yogurt

salt

1 bunch of fresh flat leaf parsley

seeds of ½ pomegranate, to garnish

SERVES 4

1 Soak eight wooden skewers in hot water for about 15 minutes, then drain. Thread one skewer through the wings of each bird and a second skewer through the legs to keep them together.

2 Place the skewered birds in a wide, shallow dish. Beat the pomegranate and lemon juice with the oil and red pepper or chilli powder, pour over the quails and rub it into the skin. Cover with foil and leave to marinate in a cold place or the refrigerator for 2–3 hours, turning the birds over from time to time.

3 Get the barbecue ready for cooking. Lift the birds out of the marinade and pour what is left of it into a bowl. Beat the yogurt into the leftover marinade and add a little salt.

4 Brush some of the yogurt mixture over the birds and place them on the prepared barbecue.

5 Cook for 4–5 minutes on each side, brushing with the yogurt as they cook to form a crust.

6 Chop some of the parsley and lay the rest on a serving dish. Place the cooked quails on the parsley and garnish with the pomegranate seeds and the chopped parsley. Serve hot.

per portion Energy 288kcal/1207kJ; Protein 37.4g; Carbohydrate 5.8g, of which sugars 5.8g; Fat 13g, of which saturates 2.7g; Cholesterol 0mg; Calcium 84mg; Fibre 0.5g; Sodium 111mg.

chicken casserole
with okra and lemon

This classic Turkish dish, *güveçte piliçli bamya*, is found in various forms throughout the Middle East. In the south-east of Anatolia, a generous dose of hot red pepper is added to give a fiery kick, otherwise it is usually mildly spiced. It is most often served on its own with chunks of bread to mop up the sauce, although it also goes well with a pilaff.

30ml/2 tbsp olive oil

30ml/2 tbsp butter

1 small free-range chicken, trimmed of excess fat and cut into quarters

2 onions, cut in half lengthways and finely sliced

2–3 garlic cloves, finely chopped

5–10ml/1–2 tsp Turkish red pepper, or 1 fresh red chilli, seeded and finely chopped

10ml/2 tsp coriander seeds

10ml/2 tsp dried oregano

5–10ml/1–2 tsp sugar

15ml/1 tbsp tomato purée (paste)

400g/14oz can chopped tomatoes

450g/1lb fresh okra, prepared as below

juice of 1 lemon

salt and ground black pepper

thick and creamy natural (plain) yogurt, to serve

SERVES 4

preparing okra *To retain colour and reduce sliminess when okra are cooked, prepare them as follows. Cut off the stalks, then place the okra in a bowl and sprinkle with 15ml/1 tbsp salt and 30–45ml/2–3 tbsp white wine vinegar or cider vinegar. Toss well and leave to sit for 1–2 hours. Rinse thoroughly and pat dry.*

1 Heat the oil with the butter in a wide, heavy pan or flameproof casserole. Add the chicken pieces and brown them on all sides. Remove from the pan and set aside.

2 Add the onions, garlic, red pepper or chilli, coriander seeds and oregano to the pan. Stir in the sugar and cook until the onions begin to colour, then stir in the tomato purée and tomatoes and add 150ml/¼ pint/⅔ cup water. Bubble up the liquid for 2–3 minutes, then slip in the chicken pieces and baste them with the sauce. Cover the pan and cook gently on top of the stove, or in the oven at 180°C/350°F/Gas 4, for about 30 minutes.

3 Sprinkle the okra over the chicken and pour the lemon juice on top. Cover the pan again and cook gently for a further 20 minutes.

4 Transfer the chicken pieces to a serving dish. Toss the okra into the tomato sauce, season with salt and pepper and spoon over and around the chicken. Serve immediately, with a bowl of yogurt on the side.

per portion Energy 386Kcal/1617kJ; Protein 47.3g; Carbohydrate 16g, of which sugars 13.1g; Fat 15.2g, of which saturates 5.7g; Cholesterol 139mg; Calcium 224mg; Fibre 7g; Sodium 181mg.

Çerkez tavuğu

This chicken and walnut dish is Circassian (*Çerkez*) in origin, but it was adopted by the Ottoman Palace chefs and became an Ottoman classic. At the height of the Ottoman Empire, young Circassian women were captured to serve as concubines to the sultans, who appreciated their renowned beauty and fair features. The true Circassian dish includes threads of fresh coriander through it, but the fine Istanbul version is famed for its pale colour, perhaps reminiscent of the fair beauties. Sometimes served as a cold *meze* dish, *çerkez tavuğu* is ideal for lunch or supper, or for a buffet spread.

1 free-range chicken, trimmed of excess fat

3 slices of day-old white bread, crusts removed

150ml/¼ pint/⅔ cup milk

175g/6oz/1½ cup shelled walnuts

4–6 garlic cloves

salt and ground black pepper

FOR THE STOCK

1 onion, quartered

1 carrot, chopped

2 celery sticks, chopped

4–6 cloves

4–6 allspice berries

4–6 black peppercorns

2 bay leaves

5ml/1 tsp coriander seeds

1 small bunch of fresh flat leaf parsley, stalks bruised and tied together

FOR THE GARNISH

30ml/2 tbsp butter

5ml/1 tsp Turkish red pepper or paprika

a few fresh coriander (cilantro) leaves

SERVES 6

1 Put the chicken into a deep pan with all of the ingredients for the stock. Pour in enough water to just cover the chicken and bring to the boil. Lower the heat, cover the pan and simmer the chicken for about 1 hour.

2 Remove the chicken from the pan and leave until cool enough to handle. Meanwhile, boil the stock with the lid off for about 15 minutes until reduced, then strain and season with salt and pepper. When the chicken has cooled a little, pull off the skin and discard it. Tear the chicken flesh into thin strips and put them into a large bowl.

3 In a shallow bowl, soak the bread in the milk for a few minutes until the milk is absorbed. Using a mortar and pestle, pound the walnuts with the garlic to form a paste, or whiz them in a blender. Beat the soaked bread into the walnut paste, then add to the chicken mixture. Now beat in spoonfuls of the warm stock to bind the chicken and walnut mixture until it is light and creamy.

4 Spoon the mixture into a serving dish, forming a smooth, rounded mound. To garnish in the Istanbul fashion, melt the butter and stir in the red pepper or paprika, then pour it in a cross shape over the mound.

5 Serve at room temperature, garnished with the coriander leaves.

per portion Energy 222kcal/937kJ; Protein 34.1g; Carbohydrate 7.6g, of which sugars 1.6g; Fat 6.4g, of which saturates 3.3g; Cholesterol 105mg; Calcium 53mg; Fibre 0.2g; Sodium 324mg.

lemon chicken thighs wrapped in aubergine

This elegant Ottoman dish is usually made with chicken thighs or veal fillet. Wrapping the meat in strips of fried aubergine may take a little time to prepare, but the result is impressive and tasty. Serve as a main course with a tomato and cucumber salad, or a salad of parsley, pepper and onion, and a buttery rice pilaff.

juice of 2–3 lemons

2 garlic cloves, crushed

4–6 allspice berries, crushed

8 chicken thighs, skinned and boned

3–4 aubergines (eggplants)

sunflower oil, for deep-frying

30ml/2 tbsp toasted flaked (sliced) almonds

1 lemon, cut into wedges, to serve

SERVES 4

1 In a shallow bowl, mix together the lemon juice, garlic and allspice berries. Toss the chicken in the mixture, rolling the pieces over in the juice to coat them thoroughly, then cover and leave to marinate in a cold place or the refrigerator for about 2 hours.

2 Using a vegetable peeler or a small, sharp knife, peel the aubergines lengthways in stripes like a zebra. Slice them thinly lengthways – you need 16 strips in total – then soak the slices in a bowl of salted cold water for about 30 minutes.

3 Preheat the oven to 180°C/350°F/ Gas 4. Drain the aubergines and squeeze out the excess water. Heat enough oil for deep-frying in a wok or other deep-sided pan, and deep-fry the aubergines in batches for 2–3 minutes until golden brown. Remove with a slotted spoon and drain on kitchen paper.

4 On a board or plate, lay two strips of aubergine over one another in a cross shape, then place a chicken thigh in the middle. Tuck the thigh into a bundle and wrap the aubergine around it.

5 Place the aubergine parcel, seam side down, in a lightly greased ovenproof dish and repeat the process with the remaining aubergine strips and chicken.

6 Pour any remaining marinade over the parcels and sprinkle with the toasted almonds. Cover with foil and bake for 35–40 minutes. Serve hot, with lemon wedges.

per portion Energy 509kcal/2114kJ; Protein 34.7g; Carbohydrate 2.7g, of which sugars 2.3g; Fat 40g, of which saturates 8.4g; Cholesterol 180mg; Calcium 67mg; Fibre 2.6g; Sodium 108mg.

SWEET SNACKS AND JAMS

baklava

Istanbul chewy ice cream

poached apricots in scented syrup
with buffalo cream

pumpkin poached in clove-infused syrup

sütlaç

ladies' navels

fresh figs baked with honey, vanilla
and cinnamon

festive semolina helva with pine nuts

kazandibi

rose petal sorbet

dried fig jam with aniseed and pine nuts

plum tomato and almond jam

140

sweet snacks and jams

Delectable, creamy puddings; sweet syrupy pastries filled
with pistachios, almonds and walnuts; rose and cherry
flavoured sorbets – these are just some of Turkey's delights.

"Eat sweet, talk sweet", say the Turks, who are
proud of their milk pudding and sweet pastry
heritage. Undoubtedly, most Turks have a sweet
tooth, and many of their syrupy pastries and
sweetmeats rank high on the scale of sweetness.
Principally enjoyed as snacks at any time of day,
rather than desserts at the end of a meal,
puddings and sweetmeats also play an important
role in Turkish culture.

When visiting a home or joining a family for a
meal, it is polite to bear a gift of something
sweet. The same custom applies when celebrating
a birth, engagement or wedding – sweet pastries,
such as *baklava*, or nut-based *helva* and rose-
flavoured *lokum* (Turkish delight) are presented as
gifts by guests or offered by the host. Even when
mourning a death, a sweet semolina *helva* is
prepared for visitors. At religious festivals, such as
the feast days called *Kandil*, and the festival at the
end of the month of fasting, *Ramazan Bayramı*
(which is also known as *Şeker Bayramı*, the

Above, from left to right
Pumpkin poached in
clove-infused syrup, sütlaç,
kazandibi.

Festival of Sweets), there is a splendid, seemingly
never-ending flow of sweet pastries, *helva* and
lokma (fried pastries in syrup). For such events
some people will drive to the other side of a city
to get the freshest and best *baklava* from the
right *baklavacı*, or the creamiest milk pudding
from the most renowned *muhallebici,* the maker
of milk puddings and delicacies like the rolls of
kaymak (clotted cream made from the milk of
water buffalos).

Perhaps enforced by the Koranic verse "to
enjoy sweets is a sign of faith", there seems no
limit to the capacity and creativity of pudding-
and sweet-making in the line of religious or social
duty. *Helva* is made to commemorate many
harvests and festivals, as well as events such as
births and deaths, moving house, graduating from
school and entering military service. *Zerde*, a jelly-
like, saffron-scented, rice pudding is traditionally
prepared for weddings and circumcision feasts,
and a pulse and grain pudding of great antiquity,
aşure is prepared between the 10th and 20th day
of *Muharram*, the first month of the Muslim
calendar. Associated with the legend of Noah's
Ark, this pudding is believed to have been created
when provisions ran low on the Ark and Noah
suggested that whatever was left should be
boiled together to feed everyone. Following

tradition, this hearty pudding is made in vast quantities and shared with friends and neighbours.

According to Islamic custom, milk is rarely drunk as a liquid but turned instead into yogurt, ice-cream and milk puddings. The *muhallebici* has been a key figure in Turkish culinary culture since Ottoman times. The industrious milk pudding chefs of the Palace kitchens created and adapted many delectable creamy dishes, including an extraordinary one made with chicken breast, *tavuk göğsü*, also known as *kazandibi* when the top is browned. Flavoured with rose water or vanilla, or with almonds as in *keşkul,* milk puddings are traditionally thickened with a rice extract called *sübye*, for which rice flour slaked with water can be substituted.

The maker of sweet pastries, the *baklavacı,* is revered just as much as the milk pudding maker. Aside from the traditional *baklava* made with thin sheets of pastry dough and chopped walnuts, there are many other specialities, including *güllaç,* paper-thin pastry sheets soaked in milk and rose water; *bülbül yuvası* (nightingale's nests) named after their shape; *sütlü nüriye,* moist layers of milky, syrup-soaked pastry filled with shaved almonds; and *kadaif* made with shredded pastry and pistachios, which can also be moulded into "young girls' breasts" (*kiz memesi kadayıf*). The

reputable pastry houses in Istanbul, Bursa and Izmir are also the best places to sample traditional fried doughs soaked in syrup, such as *hanım göbeği* (ladies' navels) and *vezir parmağı* (vizier's fingers), both creations of the Ottoman Palace.

Juicy, ripe seasonal fruits – melons, peaches, figs, pomegranates and grapes – are mainly eaten fresh, but there are several puddings that feature dried fruits, such as *hoşaf,* a refreshing compote of apricots, sultanas (golden raisins), almonds and pine nuts. Apricots and figs, dried and fresh, are often filled with cream or nuts and soaked in syrup; fresh sour cherries are cooked with sugar and poured over baked bread to make *vişneli ekmek tatlısı*; and quince and pumpkins poached in clove-scented syrup make popular desserts.

Unripe fruits are much sought after for jam, and even some unripe vegetables are destined for the syrupy conserves that are such a feature of Turkish culinary life. Ranging from delicate rose petal, whole green fig and shredded quince to succulent peach or apricot, watermelon and whole baby aubergine (eggplant), jam is served for breakfast with warm fresh bread and slabs of moist white cheese, or enjoyed as a sweet snack, drizzled over freshly baked cakes and doughs, or spooned on top of creamy yogurt. Exquisite and colourful, Turkish jams are unique – and out of this world.

Above, from left to right
Ladies' navels, fresh figs, poached apricots.

baklava

An Ottoman legacy, *baklava* is one of greatest creations from the pastry chefs at the Topkapı Palace. Traditionally made with eight layers of pastry dough and seven layers of chopped nuts, the secret, apparently, is in the specially prepared, paper-thin dough made from clarified butter and the finest flour. Generally, *baklava* is enjoyed as a mid-morning sweet snack with a cup of strong Turkish coffee, or as a mid-afternoon pick-me-up with a glass of tea.

175g/6oz/³/4 cup clarified or plain butter, or sunflower oil

100ml/3¹/2fl oz/scant ¹/2 cup sunflower oil

450g/1lb filo sheets

450g/1lb walnuts, or a mixture of walnuts, pistachios and almonds, finely chopped

5ml/1 tsp ground cinnamon

FOR THE SYRUP

450g/1lb sugar

juice of 1 lemon, or 30ml/2 tbsp rose water

SERVES 12

1   Preheat the oven to 160°C/325°F/ Gas 3. Melt the butter and oil in a small pan, then brush a little over the bottom and sides of a 30cm/12in round or square cake tin (pan). Place a sheet of filo in the bottom and brush it with melted butter and oil. Continue until you have used half the filo sheets, brushing each one with butter and oil. Ease the sheets into the corners and trim the edges if they flop over the rim of the tin.

2   Spread the nuts over the last buttered sheet and sprinkle with the cinnamon, then continue as before with the remaining filo sheets. Brush the top one as well, then, using a sharp knife, cut diagonal parallel lines right through all the layers to the bottom to form small diamond shapes.

3   Pop the *baklava* into the oven for about 1 hour, until the top is golden – if it is still pale, increase the temperature for a few minutes at the end.

4   While the *baklava* is in the oven, make the syrup. Put the sugar into a heavy pan, pour in 250ml/8fl oz/1 cup water and bring to the boil, stirring all the time.

5   When the sugar has dissolved, lower the heat and stir in the lemon juice, then simmer for about 15 minutes, until the syrup thickens. Leave to cool in the pan.

6   When the *baklava* is ready, remove it from the oven and slowly pour the cooled syrup over the piping hot pastry. Return to the oven for 2–3 minutes to soak up the syrup, then take it out and leave to cool.

7   Once the *baklava* is cool, lift the diamond-shaped pieces out of the tin and arrange them in a serving dish.

at the pastry shop *The best* baklava *is to be found in a busy, central pastry shop, where the wide selection of pastries on offer will also include the melt-in-the-mouth* sütlü nüriye, *a layered pastry filled with shaved almonds and bathed in a milky syrup; the moist, diamond-shaped* şöbiyet *filled with chopped pistachios; and the crunchy* bülbül yuvası, *a wrinkled spiral filled with nuts to resemble the nightingale's nest after which it is named.*

per portion Energy 973kcal/4059kJ; Protein 12.2g; Carbohydrate 89.9g, of which sugars 60.9g; Fat 65.2g, of which saturates 15.6g; Cholesterol 47mg; Calcium 139mg; Fibre 3.1g; Sodium 141mg.

Istanbul chewy ice cream

There are many delicious flavours of ice cream, *dondurma*, in Turkey, but one that stands out above all others is the classic chewy ice cream. A feature of Istanbul street life and ice-cream parlours, it is served from great vats using a wooden paddle. The pine-scented tree gum or mastic (*mastika*) provides the chewy consistency, while the silky, ground orchid root (*salep*) contributes to its pearly white colour as well as acting as a thickening agent.

900ml/1½ pints/3¾ cups full-fat (whole) milk

300ml/½ pint/1¼ cups double (heavy) cream

225g/8oz/generous 1 cup sugar

45ml/3 tbsp ground *salep*

1–2 pieces of *mastika* (see below), crushed with a little sugar

SERVES 4

1 Put the milk, cream and sugar into a heavy pan and bring to the boil, stirring all the time, until the sugar has dissolved. Lower the heat and simmer for 10 minutes.

2 Put the *salep* into a bowl. Moisten it with a little cold milk, add a spoonful of the hot, sweetened milk, then tip it into the pan, stirring all the time.

3 Beat the mixture gently and stir in the *mastika*, then continue simmering for 10–15 minutes.

4 Pour the liquid into a freezer container, cover with a dry dish towel and leave to cool.

5 Remove the dish towel, cover the container with foil and place it in the freezer. Leave to set, beating it at intervals to disperse the ice crystals. Alternatively, churn the cooled liquid in an ice-cream maker.

6 Before serving, allow the ice cream to sit out of the freezer for 5–10 minutes so that it becomes soft enough to scoop.

mastika This is the aromatic gum from the *pistacia lentiscus tree* that grows wild in the Mediterranean region. When sold in the markets, mastika *is in clear crystal form, often containing a few ants that managed to get caught in the sticky gum. The aroma will indicate the strength of the resinous taste, which the crystals impart to the dish along with the chewy texture. To use the crystals they must first be pulverized with a little sugar, using a mortar and pestle. In Turkey, mastika is used to give flavour and texture to the famous snowy ice cream and the Ottoman milk pudding,* muhallebi*. It also lends its chewy punch to some bread doughs, and to* rakı.

per portion Energy 742Kcal/3093kJ; Protein 8.9g; Carbohydrate 70.2g, of which sugars 70.2g; Fat 49.1g, of which saturates 30.7g; Cholesterol 134mg; Calcium 332mg; Fibre 0g; Sodium 117mg.

1 Drain the soaked apricots and pour the soaking water into a measuring jug (pitcher) up to the 250ml/8fl oz/1 cup mark (if there is not enough, make up the amount with fresh water). Pour the measured liquid into a heavy pan, add the sugar and bring to the boil, stirring all the time.

poached apricots in scented syrup with buffalo cream

A legacy of the Ottoman Empire, this dish is both simple and sophisticated. Tender apricots are poached in a light syrup scented with orange blossom water, then filled with the Turkish buffalo cream called *kaymak*. Served chilled as a sweet treat or dessert, it is deliciously sweet and refreshing.

250g/9oz/generous 1 cup dried apricots, soaked in cold water for at least 6 hours or overnight

200g/7oz/1 cup sugar

juice of 1 lemon

30ml/2 tbsp orange blossom water

225g/8oz *kaymak* (see right)

SERVES 4

kaymak Made from the milk of water buffalos, this cream is very thick, almost like clotted cream. If you cannot find it, you can fill the apricots with crème fraîche or clotted cream instead.

2 When the sugar has dissolved, boil the syrup vigorously for 2–3 minutes. Lower the heat, stir in the lemon juice and orange blossom water, then slip in the apricots and poach gently for 15–20 minutes. Leave the apricots to cool.

3 Lift an apricot out of the syrup. Pull it open with your fingers, or slit it with a knife, and fill with the *kaymak*. Place the filled apricot, cream side up, in a shallow serving dish and repeat with the remaining apricots and cream.

4 Carefully spoon the syrup around the filled apricots, so the flesh of the fruit is kept moist but the cream is not submerged. Place the dish in the refrigerator to chill before serving.

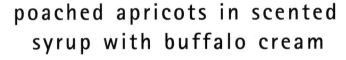

per portion Energy 333kcal/1416kJ; Protein 4.6g; Carbohydrate 77.6g, of which sugars 77.6g; Fat 2.6g, of which saturates 1.4g; Cholesterol 8mg; Calcium 139mg; Fibre 4g; Sodium 36mg.

pumpkin poached in clove-infused syrup

In winter the markets and streets are alive with busy pumpkin stalls, selling pumpkin flesh prepared especially for this exquisite dish. Serve on its own or with chilled clotted cream or crème fraîche.

450g/1lb sugar

juice of 1 lemon

6 cloves

1kg/2¼lb peeled and deseeded pumpkin flesh, cut into cubes or rectangular blocks

SERVES 4–6

1 Put the sugar into a deep, wide, heavy pan and pour in 250ml/8fl oz/ 1 cup water. Bring to the boil, stirring all the time, until the sugar has dissolved, then boil gently for 2–3 minutes.

2 Lower the heat and stir in the lemon juice and cloves, then slip in the pumpkin pieces and bring the liquid back to the boil. Lower the heat and put the lid on the pan. Poach the pumpkin gently, turning the pieces over from time to time, until they are tender and a rich, gleaming orange colour. This may take 1½–2 hours, depending on the size of the pumpkin pieces.

3 Leave the pumpkin to cool in the pan, then lift the pieces out of the syrup and place them in a serving dish.

4 Spoon most, or all, of the syrup over the pumpkin pieces and serve at room temperature or chilled.

per portion Energy 317kcal/1353kJ; Protein 1.6g; Carbohydrate 82.1g, of which sugars 81.2g; Fat 0.3g, of which saturates 0.2g; Cholesterol 0mg; Calcium 88mg; Fibre 1.7g; Sodium 5mg.

sütlaç

From the Ottoman Palace kitchens to your table at home, this is the best-ever baked rice pudding. Creamy and flavoured with vanilla, each spoonful just slips down your throat. Some traditional pudding stores burn the top of the pudding to give it a charred-looking skin, while others opt for a softer-looking, paler pudding, perhaps delicately flavoured with rose water or dusted with cinnamon.

100g/3¾ oz/½ cup short grain, or pudding rice, rinsed thoroughly and drained

2 litres/3½ pints/8 cups full-fat (whole) milk

90g/3½ oz/½ cup sugar

30ml/2 tbsp rice flour

5–10ml/1–2 tsp vanilla extract, or the seeds scraped from a juicy vanilla pod (bean)

SERVES 4–6

1 Tip the rice into a deep, heavy pan, pour in enough water to just cover the rice and bring to the boil. Lower the heat and simmer for 5–6 minutes, until the water has been absorbed.

2 Pour in the milk and bring to the boil, stirring, then lower the heat and simmer until the liquid begins to thicken.

3 Add the sugar, stirring all the time until the sugar has dissolved, then stir in the vanilla and simmer for a further 15–20 minutes. Meanwhile, preheat the oven to 200°C/400°F/Gas 6.

4 In a small bowl, moisten the rice powder with a little water to make a smooth paste. Stir in a spoonful of the hot liquid, then tip this mixture into the pan of rice, stirring all the time to prevent lumps forming.

5 Once the liquid has thickened a little, tip the mixture into an ovenproof dish and bake in the oven for about 25 minutes, until the pudding is lightly browned on top.

6 Remove the pudding from the oven and leave to cool, allowing a skin to form on top, then chill well in the refrigerator, preferably overnight.

zerde *Another popular rice pudding is zerde, which is more jelly-like than creamy. Coloured yellow with saffron and flavoured with rose water, it is traditionally served at wedding feasts.*

per portion Energy 364kcal/1520kJ; Protein 12.6g; Carbohydrate 49.7g, of which sugars 32.4g; Fat 13.1g, of which saturates 8.4g; Cholesterol 47mg; Calcium 407mg; Fibre 0.1g; Sodium 145mg.

ladies' navels

This is a classic fried pastry, an invention from the Topkapı Palace kitchens. Garnish it with whole or chopped pistachios and serve with *kaymak* (thick buffalo cream) or any other cream you like.

3 Beat the eggs into the cooled mixture so that it gleams. Add 15ml/ 1 tbsp of the cooled syrup and beat well.

4 Pour enough oil for deep-frying into a wok or other deep-sided pan. Heat until just warm, then remove the pan from the heat. Wet your hands and take an apricot-size piece of dough in your fingers. Roll it into a ball, flatten it in the palm of your hand, then use your finger to make an indentation in the middle to resemble a lady's navel.

5 Drop the dough into the pan of warmed oil. Repeat with the rest of the mixture to make about 12 navels.

6 Place the pan back over the heat. As the oil heats up, the pastries will swell, retaining the dip in the middle. Swirl the oil, until the navels turn golden all over. Remove the navels from the oil with a slotted spoon, then toss them in the cooled syrup. Leave to soak for a few minutes, arrange in a serving dish and spoon some of the syrup over.

50g/2oz/¼ cup butter

2.5ml/½ tsp salt

175g/6oz/1½ cups plain (all-purpose) flour

60g/2oz/⅓ cup semolina

2 eggs

sunflower oil, for deep-frying

FOR THE SYRUP

450g/1lb/scant 2¼ cups granulated sugar

juice of 1 lemon

SERVES 4–6

1 Make the syrup. Put the sugar and 300ml/½ pint/1¼ cups water into a heavy pan and bring to the boil, stirring all the time. When the sugar has dissolved, stir in the lemon juice and lower the heat, then simmer for about 10 minutes, until the syrup has thickened a little. Leave to cool.

2 Put the butter, salt and 250ml/8fl oz/ 1 cup water in another heavy pan and bring to the boil. Remove from the heat and add the flour and semolina, beating all the time, until the mixture becomes smooth and leaves the side of the pan. Leave to cool.

per portion Energy 517kcal/2190kJ; Protein 6.3g; Carbohydrate 108.8g, of which sugars 78.9g; Fat 9.3g, of which saturates 4.9g; Cholesterol 81mg; Calcium 93mg; Fibre 1.1g; Sodium 80mg.

fresh figs baked with honey, vanilla and cinnamon

Baking fruit with honey is an ancient cooking method, devised perhaps when local fruit harvests were so abundant there was too much to eat fresh. This is a dish most often made with apricots or figs in rural homes, where it is sometimes served as a sweet snack for everyone to share, with bread to mop up the yogurt and honey. Spices and herbs, such as aniseed, cinnamon, rosemary and lavender, are often used for flavouring. If you choose ripe figs with a sweet, pink interior, and an aromatic honey, you can't go wrong.

12 ripe figs

30ml/2 tbsp vanilla sugar (see below)

3–4 cinnamon sticks

45–60ml/3–4 tbsp clear honey

225g/8oz/1 cup chilled thick and creamy natural (plain) yogurt, clotted cream or *kaymak* (see page 146)

SERVES 3–4

1 Preheat the oven to 200°C/400°F/ Gas 6. Wash the figs and pat them dry. Using a sharp knife, cut a deep cross from the top of each fig to the bottom, keeping the skin at the bottom intact. Fan each fig out, so it looks like a flower, then place them upright in a baking dish, preferably an earthenware one.

2 Sprinkle the vanilla sugar over each fig flower, tuck in the cinnamon sticks and drizzle with honey. Bake for 15–20 minutes, until the sugar is slightly caramelized but the honey and figs are still moist.

3 Eat the figs straight away. Spoon a dollop of yogurt or cream into the middle of each one and scoop them up with your fingers, or serve them in bowls and let everyone help themselves to the yogurt or cream.

vanilla sugar *To make the vanilla sugar for this recipe, split a vanilla pod (bean) lengthways in half, scrape out the seeds and mix them with 30ml/2 tbsp caster (superfine) sugar.*

per portion Energy 198kcal/845kJ; Protein 2.3g; Carbohydrate 48.2g, of which sugars 48.2g; Fat 1g, of which saturates 0g; Cholesterol 0mg; Calcium 155mg; Fibre 4.5g; Sodium 39mg.

225g/8oz/1 cup butter

450g/1lb/scant 2¾ cups semolina

45ml/3 tbsp pine nuts

900ml/1½ pints/3¾ cups milk

225g/8oz/generous 1 cup sugar

5–10ml/1–2 tsp ground cinnamon

SERVES 6–8

festive semolina helva with pine nuts

Helva signifies good fortune and is made for events like moving house or starting a new job, but it is also traditional for the bereaved family to offer it to friends when someone dies.

1   Melt the butter in a heavy pan, stir in the semolina and pine nuts and cook over a medium heat, stirring all the time, until lightly browned.

2   Lower the heat and pour in the milk. Mix well, cover the pan with a dish towel and press the lid down tightly. Pull the flaps of the dish towel up and over the lid and simmer gently for 10–12 minutes, until the milk has been absorbed.

3   Add the sugar and stir until it has dissolved. Cover the pan with the dish towel and lid again, remove from the heat and leave to stand for 1 hour.

4   To serve, mix well with a wooden spoon and spoon into bowls, then dust with cinnamon.

per portion Energy 568kcal/2388kJ; Protein 10.2g; Carbohydrate 78.3g, of which sugars 34.7g; Fat 26g, of which saturates 15.9g; Cholesterol 67mg; Calcium 165mg; Fibre 1.2g; Sodium 227mg.

kazandibi

For the "eat sweet, talk sweet" Turks, there is one pudding above all others that they will insist you try. A classic Ottoman dish that may even have had its origins in the lavish feasting of the Romans when Anatolia was once part of its eastern empire, it emerged from the Topkapı kitchens as *tavuk göğsü*, a creamy milk pudding made with chicken breast fillets. Over time it has developed to produce the popular offshoot *kazandibi*, which is really the same pudding with a burnt top that is rolled into logs.

1 skinless, boneless chicken breast
75ml/5 tbsp rice flour
900ml/1½ pints/3¾ cups milk
300ml/½ pint/1¼ cups double (heavy) cream
a pinch of salt
175g/6oz/scant 1 cup granulated sugar
ground cinnamon, for dusting

SERVES 6

1 Place the chicken breast fillet in a pan with enough water to just cover it. Bring the water to the boil, lower the heat and simmer for 6–7 minutes, until the breast is tender. Drain the chicken and tear the meat into very fine threads.

2 In a bowl, moisten the rice flour with a little of the milk to form a smooth paste that has the consistency of double cream. Pour the rest of the milk and the cream into a heavy pan, add the salt and sugar and bring to the boil, stirring all the time, until the sugar has dissolved.

3 Add a few spoonfuls of the hot milk mixture to the moistened rice flour, then tip back into the pan and stir vigorously. Lower the heat and stir constantly until the mixture begins to thicken, then gently beat in the chicken and continue to simmer until the mixture is very thick.

4 Lightly grease a heavy frying pan and place it over the heat. When the pan is hot, tip the pudding mixture into it and keep it over the heat for 5 minutes to brown, or burn, the bottom – check by lifting up an edge to peep beneath.

5 Move the pan around to make sure the bottom is evenly burned, then turn off the heat and leave the pudding to cool in the pan.

6 Using a sharp-pointed knife, cut the pudding into rectangles. Lift each rectangle out of the pan with a palette knife or metal spatula and place on a flat surface. Roll each rectangle over so that it resembles a log, and place seam side down in a serving dish. Serve chilled or at room temperature as a sweet snack or dessert, dusted with a little cinnamon.

per portion Energy 504kcal/2107kJ; Protein 12.9g; Carbohydrate 48.4g, of which sugars 38.4g; Fat 29.8g, of which saturates 18.4g; Cholesterol 95mg; Calcium 224mg; Fibre 0.3g; Sodium 93mg.

rose petal sorbet

The ancient Egyptians, Romans, Persians and seafaring Arabs all used the rose for scenting and culinary purposes. By the time it reached the Ottoman Palace kitchens, the petals had already been used to make rose water and wine. Entranced by its perfume, the Topkapı Palace chefs splashed rose water into their syrupy pastries and milk puddings, and infused the pretty petals in syrup to make fragrant jams and sorbets. This sorbet looks lovely served in frosted glasses or fine glass bowls, decorated with fresh or crystallized rose petals – these are easy to make by brushing the petals with whisked egg white, dipping them in sugar and leaving to dry until crisp.

fresh petals of 2 gloriously scented red or pink roses, free from pesticides

225g/8oz/generous 1 cup caster (superfine) sugar

juice of 1 lemon

15ml/1 tbsp rose water

SERVES 3–4

1 Wash the rose petals and cut off the white bases. Place in a pan with 600ml/ 1 pint/2½ cups water and bring to the boil. Turn off the heat, cover the pan and leave the petals to steep for 10 minutes.

2 Strain off the water and reserve the petals. Pour the water back into the pan, add the sugar and bring to the boil, stirring, until the sugar has dissolved.

3 Boil for 1–2 minutes, then lower the heat and simmer for 5–10 minutes, until the syrup thickens a little.

4 Stir in the lemon juice, rose water and reserved petals, turn off the heat and leave the mixture to cool in the pan.

5 Pour into a freezer container and place in the freezer until beginning to set. Take the sorbet out of the freezer at 2–3 hour intervals and whisk to disperse the ice crystals. Alternatively, freeze in an electric sorbetière.

6 Before serving, take the sorbet out of the freezer for 5–10 minutes, so that it softens enough to scoop.

rose water *Clear, fragrant rose water is much prized in Turkish households. It is splashed on the face and hands to freshen up before or after a meal, and it is used to scent many sweet dishes – milky puddings, sherbet drinks, syrups, fruit salads and Turkish delight. Find it in supermarkets, health food and specialist stores.*

per portion Energy 222kcal/946kJ; Protein 0.3g; Carbohydrate 58.8g, of which sugars 58.8g; Fat 0g, of which saturates 0g; Cholesterol 0mg; Calcium 30mg; Fibre 0g; Sodium 4mg.

450g/1lb/2¼ cups granulated sugar

juice of 1 lemon

5ml/1 tsp ground aniseed

about 700g/1lb 9oz dried figs, coarsely chopped

45–60ml/3–4 tbsp pine nuts

MAKES ENOUGH FOR 3–4 X 450G/1LB JAM JARS

dried fig jam with aniseed and pine nuts

One of the classic commercial jams in Turkey is made with whole, peeled, unripe green figs that float like globes of precious jade in a pale, transparent syrup. Spooned on to fresh bread, the taste of each bite of green fig is more reminiscent of honeycomb than the fruit itself. Jars of this delectable jam are readily available in Middle Eastern stores. Less well known, but equally good, is this homemade winter jam made with dried figs and pine nuts. It is delicious spread on hot fresh bread straight from the baker's oven. Look for succulent dried figs with a springy texture – ones that are good enough to snack on – available in some supermarkets, delicatessens and health food stores.

1 Put the sugar and 600ml/1 pint/2½ cups water into a heavy pan and bring to the boil, stirring all the time, until the sugar has dissolved. Lower the heat and simmer for 5–10 minutes, until the syrup begins to thicken.

2 Stir in the lemon juice, aniseed and figs. Bring to the boil once more, then lower the heat again and simmer for 15–20 minutes, until the figs are tender.

3 Add the pine nuts and simmer for a further 5 minutes. Leave the jam to cool in the pan before spooning into sterilized jars and sealing. Stored in a cool, dry place, it will keep for several months.

per portion Energy 869kcal/3693kJ; Protein 8.4g; Carbohydrate 197.5g, of which sugars 197.5g; Fat 10.5g, of which saturates 0.5g; Cholesterol 0mg; Calcium 492mg; Fibre 13.4g; Sodium 115mg.

plum tomato and almond jam

In the style of a conserve, you will only ever come across this jam in a Turkish home, as it is not made commercially like the well-known ones made with rose petals, green figs, sour cherries or quince. A summer jam, made with slightly unripe or firm plum tomatoes, it is syrupy in consistency, and spooned, rather than spread, on to bread.

1kg/2¼lb firm plum tomatoes

500g/1¼ lb/2½ cups sugar

115g/4oz/1 cup whole blanched almonds

8–10 whole cloves

MAKES ENOUGH FOR 2–3 X 450G/1LB JAM JARS

1 Skin the tomatoes. Submerge them for a few seconds in boiling water, then plunge them straight away into a bowl of cold water. Remove them from the water one at a time and peel off the skins.

2 Place the skinned tomatoes in a heavy pan and cover with the sugar. Leave them to sit for a few hours, or overnight, to draw out some of the juices, then stir in 150ml/¼ pint/⅔ cup water. The tomatoes should be quite juicy – if not, stir in more water, you may need up to 300ml/½ pint/1¼ cups.

3 Place the pan over the heat and stir gently until the sugar has completely dissolved. Bring the syrup to the boil and boil for a few minutes, skimming off any froth, then lower the heat and stir in the almonds and cloves. Simmer gently for about 25 minutes, stirring from time to time.

4 Turn off the heat and leave the jam to cool in the pan before spooning into sterilized jars and sealing.

5 Stored in a cool, dry place, it will keep for several months, but you will probably find that you eat it almost as soon as you've made it.

per portion Energy 948Kcal/4016kJ; Protein 11.3g; Carbohydrate 187.1g, of which sugars 186.1g; Fat 22.4g, of which saturates 2g; Cholesterol 0mg; Calcium 204mg; Fibre 6.2g; Sodium 45mg.

index

A

acvar 29
Ahmet III 16
alcohol 16
allspice 71
almonds 14
   artichokes with beans and almonds 72
   plum tomato and almond jam 157
Anatolian bulgur with nuts and dates 91
Anatolian *mantı* 60
anchovies 36, 96
aniseed 156
apples stuffed with sweet rice 81
apricots
   carrot and apricot rolls with mint yogurt 75
   poached apricots in scented syrup with
      buffalo cream 146
   pumpkin stuffed with apricot and saffron
      pilaff 92
armut turşusu 13
Arnavut ciğeri 124
artichokes with beans and almonds 72
aubergines
   acvar 29
   aubergine pilaff with cinnamon and mint 95
   imam bayıldı 66
   lemon chicken thighs wrapped in aubergine
      136
   smoked aubergine and yogurt purée 24
   smoked aubergines in cheese sauce 69
ayran 12

B

baked chickpea purée with lemon and
   pine nuts 33
baked sardines with tomatoes, thyme and
   purple basil 106
baklava 142
basil 106
beans 6, 84, 85
   artichokes with beans and almonds 72
   bean salad with red onion, eggs, olives
      and anchovies 36
   black-eyed bean stew with spicy sausage 86
   green beans with tomatoes and dill 70
   zeytinyağlı barbunya 90
beer 16
   deep-fried mussels in beer batter with
      garlic-flavoured walnut sauce 55
beetroot and yogurt salad 41
beyaz peynir 11, 12
bread 14
   Çerkez tavuğu 134
   lahmacun 59
   pide 15
   yogurtlu şiş kebab 129
bulgur 84
   Anatolian bulgur with nuts and dates 91
   kısır 27

C

caramelized mushrooms with allspice
   and herbs 71
carrots
   carrot and apricot rolls with mint yogurt 75
   carrot and caraway purée with yogurt 28
   garlic-flavoured lentils with carrots and sage 89
celebrations 9
celery and coconut salad with lime 38
Çerkez tavuğu 134
chargrilled quails in pomegranate marinade 131
chargrilled sardines in vine leaves 104
cheese 11, 12
   filo cigars filled with feta, parsley, mint
      and dill 56
   gypsy salad with feta, chillies and parsley 37
   kabak mucver 77
   leek soup with feta, dill and paprika 50
   potatoes baked with tomatoes, olives, feta
      and oregano 76
   smoked aubergines in cheese sauce 69
cherry pilaff 99
chicken 121

Çerkez tavuğu 134
chicken casserole with okra and lemon 133
kazandibi 152
lemon chicken thighs wrapped in aubergine
   136
chickpeas 85
   Anatolian *mantı* 60
   chickpea purée with lemon and pine
      nuts 33
   sultan's chickpea pilaff 98
chillies 7, 10–11
   gypsy salad with feta, chillies and parsley 37
çılbır 53
cinnamon
   aubergine pilaff with cinnamon and mint 95
   cinnamon fishcakes with currants, pine
      nuts and herbs 111
   fresh figs baked with honey, vanilla and
      cinnamon 150
   meatballs with pine nuts and cinnamon 125
cloves 147
coconut and celery salad with lime 38
coffee 16–17
çöp şiş 122
courgettes and peaches with pine nuts 78
currants 14
   cinnamon fishcakes with currants, pine nuts
      and herbs 111
   elma dolması 81
   stir-fried spinach with currants, pine nuts
      and yogurt 34

D

dates and nuts with bulgur 91
deep-fried mussels in beer batter with
   garlic-flavoured walnut sauce 55
dill 50, 56, 70
dried fig jam with aniseed and pine nuts 156
drinks 16–17
   ayran 12
   düğün çorbası 51

E

eggs
   bean salad with red onion, eggs, olives
      and anchovies 36
   çılbır 53
   menemen 52
elma dolması 81
equipment 15
etiquette 9

F
festivals 9
festive semolina helva with pine nuts 151
feta 37, 50, 56, 76, 77
figs
    dried fig jam with aniseed and pine nuts 156
    fresh figs baked with honey, vanilla and
        cinnamon 150
filo cigars filled with feta, parsley, mint and
    dill 56
fish 6, 102–3
    baked sardines with tomatoes, thyme and
        purple basil 106
    bean salad with red onion, eggs, olives and
        anchovies 36
    chargrilled sardines in vine leaves 104
    cinnamon fishcakes with currants, pine nuts
        and herbs 111
    hamsili pilav 96
    kiliç şiş 107
    mackerel *pilaki* 109
    sea bass baked in salt 110
    uskumru dolması 113
fruit 6, 81

G
garlic 55
garlic-flavoured lentils with carrots and sage 89
grated beetroot and yogurt salad 41
green beans with tomatoes and dill 70
gypsy salad with feta, chillies and parsley 37

H
hamsili pilav 96
healthy eating 7, 65
herbs 71, 111
honey 14
    fresh figs baked with honey, vanilla and
        cinnamon 150
hot snacks 44–5

I
imam bayıldı 66
Islam 6–7, 9, 16, 120, 140
Istanbul chewy ice cream 145

J
jams 141
    dried fig jam with aniseed and pine nuts 156
    plum tomato and almond jam 157

K
kabak mucver 77
karides güveç 115

kazandibi 152
kebabs 7
    yoğurtlu şiş kebab 129
kiliç şiş 107
kısır 27

L
ladies' navels 149
lahmacun 59
lamb 120
    Arnavut ciğeri 124
    çöp şiş 122
    düğün çorbası 51
    lahmacun 59
    lamb cutlets with tomato sauce 130
    meatballs with pine nuts and cinnamon 125
    vine leaves stuffed with lamb and rice 126
    yoğurtlu şiş kebab 129
leeks 7
leek soup with feta, dill and paprika 50
lemon
    baked chickpea purée with lemon and pine
        nuts 33
    chicken casserole with okra and lemon 133
    lemon chicken thighs wrapped in aubergine 136
lentils 6, 85
    garlic-flavoured lentils with carrots and sage 89
    spicy red lentil soup with onion and parsley 47

M
mackerel
    mackerel *pilaki* 109
    uskumru dolması 113
maize 7
mantı 60
mastika 14, 145
meadow yogurt soup with rice and mint 46
meat 6, 120–1
meatballs with pine nuts and cinnamon 125
Mediterranean squid with olives and red wine 114
Mehmet II 7
menemen 52
meze 20–1
mint 46, 56, 75, 95
muhammara 30
mushrooms with allspice and herbs 71
mussels in beer batter with garlic-flavoured
    walnut sauce 55
mussels stuffed with aromatic pilaff and pine
    nuts 117

N
nuts 14
    Anatolian bulgur with nuts and dates 91

O
oils 6, 11
okra and lemon chicken casserole 133
olives 11
    bean salad with red onion, eggs, olives and
        anchovies 36
    Mediterranean squid with olives and red
        wine 114
    potatoes baked with tomatoes, olives, feta
        and oregano 76
onions 36
oregano 76
Ottoman Empire 6, 7, 65

P
parsley 37, 47, 56
peaches and courgettes with pine nuts 78
pears
    armut turşusu 13
peppers 7, 10–11
    acvar 29
    kiliç şiş 107
    menemen 52
    taze ezmesi 22
pickles 13
pide 15
pilaffs 7, 84–5
    aubergine pilaff with cinnamon and mint 95
    hamsili pilav 96
    mussels stuffed with aromatic pilaff and pine
        nuts 117
    pumpkin stuffed with saffron and apricot
        pilaff 92
    sour cherry pilaff 99
    sultan's chickpea pilaff 98

rose water 14
Rumi, Mevlana Celaleddin 7

S
saffron 14, 92
salads 201
salt 6
   sea bass baked in salt 110
sardines in vine leaves 104
sardines with tomatoes, thyme and purple
   basil 106
sausage and black-eyed bean stew 86
sea bass baked in salt 110
Seljuk Empire 6, 10, 65
semolina helva with pine nuts 151
shellfish 6, 103
   deep-fried mussels in beer batter with
      garlic-flavoured walnut sauce 55
   karides güveç 115
   Mediterranean squid with olives and red
      wine 114
   mussels stuffed with aromatic pilaff and
      pine nuts 117
smoked aubergine and yogurt purée 24
smoked aubergines in cheese sauce 69
snacks 44–5, 140–1
soups 44–5
sour cherry pilaff 99
spicy red lentil soup with onion and parsley 47
spicy sausage and black-eyed bean stew 86
spinach 7
   stir-fried spinach with currants, pine nuts and
      yogurt 34
sultan's chickpea pilaff 98
sumac 14
sütlaç 148
sweet snacks 44–5, 140–1
syrups 146, 147

T
tahin tarama 23
taze ezmesi 22
tea 16
thyme 106
tomatoes 7
   baked sardines with tomatoes, thyme and
      purple basil 106
   green beans with tomatoes and dill 70
   lamb cutlets with tomato sauce 130
   menemen 52
   plum tomato and almond jam 157
   potatoes baked with tomatoes, olives, feta
      and oregano 76
   taze ezmesi 22

pine nuts 14
   baked chickpea purée with lemon and pine
      nuts 33
   cinnamon fishcakes with currants, pine nuts
      and herbs 111
   dried fig jam with aniseed and pine nuts 156
   festive semolina helva with pine nuts 151
   meatballs with pine nuts and cinnamon 125
   mussels stuffed with aromatic pilaff and pine
      nuts 117
   roasted courgettes and peaches with pine
      nuts 78
   stir-fried spinach with currants, pine nuts and
      yogurt 34
pistachios 14
plum tomato and almond jam 157
poached apricots in scented syrup with buffalo
   cream 146
pomegranates
   chargrilled quails in pomegranate marinade
      131
   pomegranate broth 48
potatoes baked with tomatoes, olives, feta and
   oregano 77
pumpkin poached in clove-infused syrup 147
pumpkin stuffed with saffron and apricot pilaff 92

Q
quails 121
   chargrilled quails in pomegranate marinade 131

R
rakı 16, 20
rice 84–5
   elma dolması 81
   meadow yogurt soup with rice and mint 46
   sütlaç 148
   vine leaves stuffed with lamb and rice 126
roasted courgettes and peaches with pine nuts 78
rose petal sorbet 155

Turkish coffee 17
Turkish cuisine 6–7
   culture 8–9
   drinks 16–17
   ingredients 10–14
   meze 20–1
   utensils 15
turnips 7

U
uskumru dolması 113

V
vanilla 14
   fresh figs baked with honey, vanilla and
      cinnamon 150
vegetables 6, 7, 64–5, 81
   kabak mucver 77
vine leaves 14
   chargrilled sardines in vine leaves 104
   vine leaves stuffed with lamb and rice 126

W
walnuts 14
   Çerkez tavuğu 134
   deep-fried mussels in beer batter with
      garlic-flavoured walnut sauce 55
   muhammara 30
wine 16
   Mediterranean squid with olives and red
      wine 114

Y
Yin and Yang 7, 10, 65
yogurt 12–13
   ayran 12
   carrot and apricot rolls with mint yogurt 75
   carrot and caraway purée with yogurt 28
   grated beetroot and yogurt salad 41
   meadow yogurt soup with rice and mint 46
   smoked aubergine and yogurt purée 24
   stir-fried spinach with currants, pine nuts and
      yogurt 34
   yoğurtlu şiş kebab 129

Z
zeytinyağlı barbunya 90

PICTURE ACKNOWLEDGEMENTS
The publisher would like to thank the following
for the use of their pictures in the book (l=left,
r=right, t=top, b=bottom). **Alamy:** 8t; 9b; 11b;
12t; 14t; 14b; 17tl. **Lucy Doncaster:** 7t; 10b.
Robert Harding: 6t; 7b; 8b. **Rob Highton:** 6b.